Behold, I Have Given You a Choice

I have given you a choice to live by the truth of My Word, or to live by the knowledge of this world.

By Peter Arbib / Sound Wisdom Publications ®
Copyright 2019

https://soundwisdompublications.com/

Deuteronomy 11:26-28 KJV
26 Behold, I set before you this day a blessing and a curse;
27 A blessing, if ye obey the commandments of the LORD your God, which I command you this day:
28 And a curse, if ye will not obey the commandments of the LORD your God, ...

Jeremiah 7:23 KJV
23 But this thing commanded I them, saying, Obey my voice, and I will be your God, and ye shall be my people: and walk ye in all the ways that I have commanded you, that it may be well unto you.

2 John 1:5-6 KJV
5 ... but that which we had from the beginning, that we love one another.
6 And this is love, that we walk after his commandments. This is the commandment, That, as ye have heard from the beginning, ye should walk in it.

Matthew 22:37-39 KJV
37 Jesus said unto him, Thou shalt love the Lord thy God with all thy heart, and with all thy soul, and with all thy mind.

38 This is the first and great commandment.
39 And the second is like unto it, Thou shalt love thy neighbour as thyself.

1 Corinthians 13:13 KJV
13 And now abideth faith, hope, charity, these three; but the greatest of these is charity. *(love)*.

Colossians 2:6-7 KJV
6 As ye have therefore received Christ Jesus the Lord, *so* walk ye in him:
7 Rooted and built up in him, and stablished in the faith, as ye have been taught, abounding therein with thanksgiving.

Behold, I Have Given You A Choice

God has given you a choice to live by the truth of His Word, or to live by the knowledge of this world.

Copyright © 2019 Peter Laurence Arbib / DBA Sound Wisdom Publications ®

1st Published 03/2019
2nd Revised Edition 10/2019

All rights reserved. This book or any portion thereof may not be reproduced or used in any manner whatsoever without the express written permission from the author, except for the use of brief quotations in a book review with proper credit cited.

Published by Sound Wisdom Publications ®
Mooresville, Indiana 46158
https://SoundWisdomPublications.com

Library of Congress Catalog Number:
International Standard Book Number:
ISBN-13: 978-1723351310
ISBN-10: 1723351318

All Biblical quotations unless otherwise noted are from the King James Version of the Bible.

Words that I am researching in Scripture quotations will be marked like this **word** or **this** to help you readily see words. I will also use other comparable ways of highlighting words or phrases that are important to see, such as connected words or phrases.

Special thanks to Rev. Jon O. Nessle for his encouragement to write with the inspiration I am given on various aspects of Christian living.

Preface

2John 1:5-6 KJV
5 And now I beseech thee, lady, not as though I wrote a new commandment unto thee, but that which we had from the beginning, that we love one another.
6 And this is love, that we walk after his commandments. This is the commandment, That, as ye have heard from the beginning, ye should walk in it.

Ephesians 3:7-9 KJV
7 Whereof I was made a minister, according to the gift of the grace of God given unto me by the effectual working of his power.
8 Unto me, who am less than the least of all saints, is this grace given, that I should preach among the Gentiles the unsearchable riches of Christ;
9 And to make all *men* see what *is* the fellowship of the mystery, which from the beginning of the world hath been hid in God, who created all things ~~by Jesus Christ:~~

(The words "by Jesus Christ" were added by many translators and are omitted in the texts). [1] *And should read: <u>Eph. 3:9 "And to make all men see what is the fellowship of the mystery, which from the beginning of the world hath been hid in God, who created all things.</u>"*

From the very beginning of the creation, God has declared His love by providing everything we need to prosper and be in health. The Earth was made for mankind to live on, the animals, trees, plants, mountains, rivers, fish and so on, are for man to have food and protection. When God finally made, formed, and created man, the Earth had everything man needed. God also gave man spirit that allowed man not only to have power and dominion over the Earth and all the creatures, but to have a vital and close relationship with God. God has always provided for mankind from the beginning. This is God's love towards mankind, the same love He wants us to give to others.

3John 1:2 KJV
2 Beloved, I wish above all things that thou mayest prosper and be in health, even as thy soul prospereth.

---

[1] Bullinger E.W. *(The Companion Bible),* Zondervan Bible Publishers, Grand Rapids, Michigan. p. 1764, ref: Eph. 3:9 notes.

In the Garden of Eden, there was food, there was also perfect health provided by God that He gave to Adam and Eve. God gave them spirit, a way to communicate with God, and the ability to have fellowship *(or a relationship)* with Him, plus to have power and dominion over the Earth and its creatures.

But there was also one condition for Adam and Eve to continue in this paradise, that condition was that they could *not* eat of the tree of knowledge, of good and evil, or God would take back the spirit along with the power and dominion and fellowship they had with Him. Eve was deceived from God's arch enemy Satan and Adam had no choice but to accept that fact that Eve had already sealed their fate by her disobedience. God had no choice but to take back the spirit that He gave them. This gift of spirit was their connection with God, so they could talk with God and have a vital relationship with Him and have power and dominion over the Earth and the creatures therein.

> **Revelation 12:7-9 KJV**
> **7 And there was war in heaven: Michael and his angels fought against the dragon; and the dragon fought and his angels,**
> **8 And prevailed not; neither was their place found any more in heaven.**

9 And the great dragon was cast out, that old serpent, called the Devil, and Satan, which deceiveth the whole world: he was cast out into the earth, and his angels were cast out with him.

Genesis 2:7-9 KJV
7 And the LORD God formed man *of* the dust of the ground, and breathed into his nostrils the breath of life; and man became a living soul.
8 And the LORD God planted a garden eastward in Eden; and there he put the man whom he had formed.
9 And out of the ground made the LORD God to grow every tree that is pleasant to the sight, and good for food; the tree of life also in the midst of the garden, and the tree of knowledge of good and evil.

Genesis 2:21-23 KJV
21 And the LORD God caused a deep sleep to fall upon Adam, and he slept: and he took one of his ribs, and closed up the flesh instead thereof;
22 And the rib, which the LORD God had taken from man, made he a woman, and brought her unto the man.
23 And Adam said, This *is* now bone of my bones, and flesh of my flesh: she

shall be called Woman, because she was taken out of Man.

Genesis 1:26-28 KJV
26 And God said, Let us make man in our image, *(spirit)* **after our likeness:** *(spirit)* **and let them have dominion over the fish of the sea, and over the fowl of the air, and over the cattle, and over all the earth, and over every creeping thing that creepeth upon the earth.** *(It was through man's spirit from God that man had dominion over all the creatures on the Earth).*
27 So God created man in his *own* **image,** *(spirit)* **in the image of God created he him;** *(spirit)* **male and female created he them.**
28 And God blessed them, and God said unto them, Be fruitful, and multiply, and replenish the earth, and subdue it: and have dominion *(because of the spirit God gave them)* **over the fish of the sea, and over the fowl of the air, and over every living thing that moveth upon the earth.**

Genesis 3:1-5 KJV
1 Now the serpent *(Satan, who was cast out of heaven and placed on earth with no dominion or power over the earth)* **was more subtil than any beast of the field which**

the LORD God had made. And he said unto the woman, Yea, hath God said, Ye shall not eat of every tree of the garden?
2 And the woman said unto the serpent, We may eat of the fruit of the trees of the garden:
3 But of the fruit of the tree which *is* in the midst of the garden, God hath said, Ye shall not eat of it, neither shall ye touch it, lest ye die.
4 And the serpent said unto the woman, Ye shall not surely die:
5 For God doth know that in the day ye eat thereof, then your eyes shall be opened, and ye shall be as gods, knowing good and evil.

Genesis 3:13-15 KJV
13 And the LORD God said unto the woman, What *is* this *that* thou hast done? And the woman said, The serpent beguiled me, and I did eat.
14 And the LORD God said unto the serpent, Because thou hast done this, thou *art* cursed above all cattle, and above every beast of the field; upon thy belly shalt thou go, and dust shalt thou eat all the days of thy life:
15 And I will put enmity between thee and the woman, and between thy seed

and her seed; it shall bruise thy head, and thou shalt bruise his heel.

Satan, who along with one third of the angels were cast out of heaven because he tried to overthrow God's throne. He was the angel of light, God's "#1," second in command. But greed and jealously deteriorated Satan's motivations from love to hate, and that was his downfall. Satan did not start off with the dominion on the Earth because that was given to Adam as part of God providing everything for Adam and Eve *(mankind)* to prosper. Therefore, Satan had to deceive Adam and Eve for that dominion to be transferred to him. Satan knew that if Adam and Eve (mankind) had the dominion over him, he could not deceive mankind or attack mankind to destroy mankind.

After Satan deceived Eve, and after God took away His gift of spirit from Adam and Eve and transferred Adam's dominion to Satan, then God started *the restoration plan of the ages* to restore everything that Satan stole, and to restore the gift of spirit that God had to take back, *(Adam's spiritual power and dominion including power and dominion over Satan)*. But this time instead of restoring it immediately, mankind had to obey and believe God's Word, and the promise of the one that would restore everything. **This restoration had to be initiated by man's freedom of will, with love for God in their lifestyle.**

Mankind had to trust and believe and act on God's promises over Satan's lies.

Jesus Christ, *(God's restoration plan of the ages)* taught people how to love God, and how to love others with God's love. His mission was not only to fulfil the Law, but also to restore the hearts of God's people to live under a larger law *(living in the "spirit" of the Law)*: the law of love. This is what His teachings were about in the many parables He taught, and those that had the heart to learn came to an understanding of the parables so they could live in God's love.

Even after Jesus Christ fulfilled the law, by dying, being was raised from the dead and ascending to the right hand of his Father, God, there was much work still to be done. When we received the promise of the gift of holy spirit that also restored the dominion over the Earth *(including over Satan)*. God had provided what He had promised to Adam and Eve in Jesus Christ with a twist. It was this twist that needed to be revealed and connected to living in God's love as a spiritual family with God the creator as their Father also.

The twist was that every believer has the same amount of God's spirit in them, **and** it is unconditional, **and** it is permanent, **and** it is seed,

and[2] they are all <u>part of "the one body in Christ,"</u> <u>the family of God</u>. Satan can no longer deceive you so you could lose it, it is "eternal life" *(God's perspective)*, it is "everlasting life" *(man's perspective)*. Every believer has the same power and dominion over Satan and the Earth. It was all reinstated just as Adam and Eve originally had before the disobedience, and then some within the gift holy spirit. When we utilize that gift in any situation to receive God's deliverance and blessings, Satan's power over our life is unfulfilled and we have claimed back dominion over Satan in that situation.

Paul, who killed the new Christians as a prominent religious leader for a legalistic sect of the Jews, a Pharisee, was confronted personally by the ascended Christ and was converted. Paul was told that he was the chosen one to teach the Gentiles the "unsearchable riches of Christ," and to make all men see the "fellowship of the mystery" which was hidden in God from the beginning. What Paul revealed in the Church Epistles was the greatest redemption plan ever, and he revealed how we could live in God's love and utilize God's power from His gift of holy spirit that not only reinstated

---

[2] Bullinger, E.W. *(Figures of Speech used in the Bible)*, Baker Book House, Grand Rapids, Michigan.16th printing 1991. **"Polysyndeton" or Many Ands.** p. 208. Def: *The repetition of the word "and" at the beginning of successive clauses…. When He (God) uses "many ands"… we are asked to stop at each point, to weigh each matter that is presented to us and consider each particular that is thus added and emphasized.*

what Adam and Eve lost but added more capabilities in the category of prayer.[3]

Paul taught the same teachings as Jesus Christ did, but he added how it all fits together with God's gift of holy spirit and how the new born-again believers living as a spiritual family will also be together for eternity after the return of Christ. Jesus Christ and Paul and the other Apostles only had the Old Testament for a resource of God's Word, plus any revelation they received from God via the gift holy spirit. So, the "Christian" Principles they taught were mainly from the Old Testament writings. The main difference is that Jesus Christ fulfilled the Law to redeem us as God had revealed in bits and pieces in each book in the Bible.

That's right, each book in the Bible reveals a part of our redeemer's mission, His purpose in God's master plan to get back what was stolen from Adam and Eve. Many Christians call this "The Red Thread" that ties the whole Bible together with one major topic, God's greatest plan for the redemption of mankind. Here is the verse in Genesis that defines who and what the redeemer will accomplish in defeating Satan.

---

[3] Arbib, Peter., *(20+ Benefits Speaking in Tongues Has for You)*, Sound Wisdom Publications, Camby, IN. 2018

Genesis 3:15 KJV
15 And I *(God)* **will put enmity** *(separation)* **between thee** *(Satan)* **and the woman, and between thy seed** *(Satan's)* **and her seed;** *(God would create a perfect seed in a woman)* **it shall bruise thy head,** *(that seed would separate mankind from Satan's hold)* **and thou** *(Satan)* **shalt bruise his heel.** *(temporarily injure the promised seed though death, but God would raise Him from dead 72 hours later).*

This is the first mention of God's greatest plan of redemption in the Bible. Jesus Christ would be the enemy of Satan, and He would defeat Satan, claiming back through His obedience by his choice through his freedom of will what Adam and Eve lost by their disobedience through their choice by their freedom of will. Jesus Christ would be 100% a man, God created a perfect seed *(sperm)* in a woman to satisfy the legality that the redeemer had to be 100% man. Because it was a 100% man that disobeyed God to begin with.

There are many directions I can take this study when looking at the many topics that can be included with the different categories that can be associated with the phrase **"from the beginning."** This study will concentrate on how God has always provided everything needed for mankind to prosper and be in health throughout history. It will cover God's greatest plan for man's redemption to get back what was stolen from Adam and Eve.

But the bulk of this book will revolve around what man needs to do in response to what God has done for man, so man can once again have a vital and personal relationship with God. This is one of the largest areas of teaching in the New Testament written mainly by Paul, *the renewed mind*. This is the main topic that is connected to the phrase **"from the beginning"** in a few categories. God has always provided for mankind, even from the formation of the heavens and Earth, God was preplanning for man's existence.

This book will be a little different than my previous books where I take a verse and do a few word studies of key words or phrases from the Greek or Hebrew. This book will look at the phrase **"from the beginning"** and look at surrounding context it is used in and expand on that as the major topic.

This phrase is used in these major themes that surround it. Each chapter will expound on these themes. The numbering will correspond with the chapter numbering.

FROM THE BEGINNING:

1) God will supply and cause the Earth to supply what we need to live on the land, with the condition of "keeping" God's Word in their lifestyle. *(meet our needs by the renewed mind)*
2) God wanted us to be a part of His family spiritually, and to live within His Word to have the greatest blessings. *(be a vital part of His family by the renewed mind)*
3) God has chosen us to salvation, and to make us sons spiritually permanently and forever. *(God has saved us by our first act of the renewed mind, believing in Jesus Christ as Lord, and that he was raised from the dead)*
4) God has wanted to have fellowship, or a vital and personal relationship with mankind and with His son. *(Our relationship grows by our continual renewing of our mind)*
5) God has wanted our love, and that we love each other with His love. *(To love God, is to renew our mind to live His Word)*

From Chapter 6 on, I will be teaching on the practical side of how to renew our minds by looking at various phrases that Paul used *(chapter 6:a,b,c,d)* to convey the choice we have to either do God's Word, or to succumb to the schemes *(corrupt attitude and actions)* that originate from Satan to cause us to go against God's Word *(chapter 7:a,b)*. Plus, other topics of related interest. I will reveal keys that will help us stay focused on our primary goal to live God's Word as Jesus Christ lived God's Word towards others and the family of believers. It is not just applying knowledge, it also having the right attitude and heart in our application of God's Word. Jesus Christ not only taught the knowledge of God's Word, but also the heart, the spirit of God's Word. This is our goal also; to live God's Word in knowledge and heart!

Table of Contents

Behold, I Have Set Before You a Choice i

Preface i

1: *From the beginning: what we think and act on is our key* 1

2: *Paul's ministry: to teach "The fellowship of the mystery"* 28

3: *God's Choice and Our Choice* 56

4: *Our fellowship is with the Father and with the Son* 68

    4a: REPETITIONS, VERSE STRUCTURE, & PHRASE PAIRS .. 85
        4a:1 Verse Structure in Out Line Form 88
        4a:2 Repetitions 91
        4a:3 Similar phrases 94
        4a:4 Like Phrases or Connected Phrases 102

5: *That which we heard from the beginning, that we should love one another.* 105

6: *How to apply God's Word: The renewed mind: Key Words* 127

    6a: PUT ON 128
    6b: LET US 142
    6c: BESEECH 151
    6d: WILLING MIND 173

7: *The renewed mind: We choose who to believe* ... 185

    7a: BE NOT CONFORMED(G4964-v) TO THIS WORLD 193

7b: BUT BE YE TRANSFORMED(G3339-v) BY THE
RENEWING(G342-n) OF YOUR MIND(G3563-N) 204

8: Walking in God's Word = Walking in the renewed mind = Walking in God's love 233

 8a: RISE, WALK, PRAISING, AND LEAPING 234

 8b: WALKING IN DARKNESS, WALKING IN THE LIGHT 240

 8c: ENCOURAGEMENT: TALK THE WALK; WALK THE TALK
 248

 8d: HOW TO: TALK THE WALK AND WALK THE TALK 252

 8e: WALKING IN GOD'S LOVE = WALKING IN GOD'S WORD = WALKING IN THE RENEWED MIND 260

Confirm Your Calling as the Elect of God 270

Works Cited 278

1: From the beginning: what we think and act on is our key

Many times, when working a specific word or phrase from the Greek or Hebrew concordances I will find different topics, or categories that I can list as separate divisions of understanding, and still maintain the integrity of the base definition of the word or phrase. As we investigate some of these places "from the beginning" is used, I will note the different categories that the remoter context suggests. Right now, the exact meaning of the phrase is not a part of this study, because I will bring to your attention the categories that are introduced as a part of this study. My chapter titles will reflect one of the categories that this phrase is used in while studying it in the New Testament.

In the first use of this phrase, in the Old Testament, God is letting his people know that the land they are about to possess is not like Egypt but is a land of hills (a) valleys. Despite this, God tells them that if they hearken unto His Word, and Love Him, and serve Him, He will provide rain for the crops at the right seasons and provide grass for the cattle from the beginning of the year to the end of the year *(i.e., all year round)*. So, God will provide what is needed so they can have food. Chapter 10 reminds Israel of the exodus with Moses and how God provided for them as they moved towards the promised land. This is still true today for any individual or community that decides to live by the teachings of God's Word.

> Deuteronomy 11:10-15 KJV
> 10 For the land, whither thou goest in to possess it, *is* not as the land of Egypt, from whence ye came out, where thou sowedst thy seed, and wateredst *it* with thy foot, as a garden of herbs:
> 11 But the land, whither ye go to possess it, *is* a land of hills and valleys, *and* drinketh water of the rain of heaven:
> 12 A land which the LORD thy God careth for: the eyes of the LORD thy God *are* always upon it, <mark>from the beginning</mark> of the year even unto the end of the year.
> 13 And it shall come to pass, if ye shall hearken diligently unto my commandments which I command you this day, to love the LORD your God, and to serve him with all your heart and with all your soul,
> 14 <u>That I will give</u>(H5414) *you* the rain of your land in his due season, the first rain and the latter rain, that thou mayest gather in thy corn, and thy wine, and thine oil.

15 And I will send(H5414) **grass in thy fields for thy cattle, that thou mayest eat and be full.**

In verse 13 God gives the conditions that they need to meet so God can bless them with rain and grass to grow their crops and feed their cattle. These conditions are nothing new, but indeed they are conditions from the beginning, and finally written down and taught by Moses. These conditions are still valid today, and still hold true, and God will still honor His promise to provide our famers with the right conditions to have a good harvest and to provide for the cattle also.

Deuteronomy 11:13 conditions
1. Harken diligently unto God's Word
2. Love the Lord your God
3. Serve God with all your heart and all your soul (i.e., with all your being)

CATEGORIES:
- God will provide food for His people

In verses 14 and 15 God gives them His promise if the conditions are met. There is a repetition that is worth mentioning at the beginning of verses 14 and

15,[4] the phrases "**That I will give**" and "**And I will send**" are the same Hebrew word: nâthan (H5414) and means **to give, to send, to deliver**.[5] But because in this section God is talking in the first person, the added words "*...I will*" are properly supplied. The repetition puts the emphasis on the repeated phrase: **I will give**, or **I will send** that is, God will supply their need, so they can have food to eat. Which does not contradict His promise, but it establishes His promise. This section of Deuteronomy is about reminding His people of all the great things that He has done for them and how important it is to keep His Word burning in their hearts, and not to be deceived from other gods, that will cause them not to walk in His Word.

Repetitions tell us what the main topic is in a section. And the check on that is that the surrounding context (*you may need to go backward and/or forward a chapter or two*) corresponds with what the emphasized topics the repetitions are bringing to our attention.

---

[4] Bullinger, E.W. *(Figures of Speech used in the Bible)*, Baker Book House, Grand Rapids, Michigan. 16th printing 1991. p. 199, ref: **Anaphora; or like sentence beginnings.** ... it is repeating of the same word at the beginning of successive clauses: thus, adding weight and emphasis to statements and arguments by calling special attention to them.

[5] Strong, James. *(The New Strong's Exhaustive Concordance of the Bible)*, Thomas Nelson Publishers. 1996. Hebrew Dictionary: p. 97, ref: 5414

Between Chapter 10 and 11 there are 6 verses that repeat the same gist or meaning, just put differently. Then there are 3 verses that tell us how to implement the 6 verses of similar meaning. I brought this to our attention because when we see this many similar phrases in a small section, God is showing us that this is an important concept. It would only make sense that there would be a few verses that show us how to implement this precept in our daily lives.

That brings me to the direction I am going with this chapter. How does God provide for mankind? This chapter provides us with the answers, God is not "The Lone Ranger" in this case, but shows us that there are things that we can do on our part so God can provide what he has promised us on his part. Therefore, I am bringing out the principles of the renewed mind that is explained in the New Testament. If we want God to supply our need then we're going to, by necessity, change the way we see things and act according to God's Word in our lifestyles. Let's look at those 6 verses that have a similar concept.

> **Deuteronomy 10:12-13 KJV**
> **12** And now, Israel, what doth the LORD thy God require of thee, but <u>to fear</u> *(respect)* the LORD thy God, <u>to walk</u> in all his ways, and <u>to love him</u>, and <u>to</u>

<u>serve</u> the LORD thy God with all thy heart and with all thy soul,
13 <u>To keep the commandments</u> of the LORD, <u>and his statutes,</u> which I command thee this day for thy good?
Deuteronomy 10:20 KJV
20 Thou shalt <u>fear</u> *(respect)* the LORD thy God; him shalt thou <u>serve,</u> and to him shalt thou <u>cleave,</u> and <u>swear</u> *(take an oath)* by his name.

Deuteronomy 11:1 KJV
1 Therefore thou shalt <u>love</u> the LORD thy God, and <u>keep</u> his charge, and his statutes, and his judgments, and his commandments, alway.

Deuteronomy 11:8 KJV
8 Therefore shall ye <u>keep</u> all the commandments which I command you this day, that ye may be strong, and go in and possess the land, whither ye go to possess it;

Deuteronomy 11:16 KJV
16 <u>Take heed</u> to yourselves, that your heart be not deceived, and ye turn aside, and serve other gods, and worship them;

Deuteronomy 11:32 KJV

32 And ye shall <u>observe to do</u> all the statutes and judgments which I set before you this day.

Let's look at the things that I have underlined in the previous verses and take a look at this list of things that are mentioned for us as guidance on keeping God's Word in our hearts. What is fascinating is that when you start looking at a section closely you start to see things like a list or several verses that say the same thing just in a separate way. Then when you notice a list you can write those down one after the other and get a great summary of what is mentioned. If there is a duplicate, I will not list it a second time, unless a different context is mentioned.

Something that my minister has taught me is that when lists are mentioned in sections of scripture, they help define that section and give you the practical application that God wants you to understand. Lists are also a failsafe to rightly dividing that section without interjecting your own personal opinions, or private interpretation.

1. D10:12: **fear:** respect, honor, in the Hebrew
2. D10:12: **walk:** a manner of life, used figuratively
3. D10:12 **love:** love towards God
4. D10:12: **serve:** to do work, or to do the work of God

    a. How? D10:12: **with all they heart, and all they soul:** With all your mind and with all your life.
- 5. D10:13: **keep:** (H8104) *(His commandments)* to guard, to watch, to protect, to give heed
- 6. D10:20: **cleave:** to cling, stay close, stick with or to
- 7. D10:20: **swear:** to take an oath, to be obliged or compelled to respect and served God, in the Hebrew
- 8. D11:1: **keep:** (H8104) *(your service or obligation)* to guard, to watch, to protect, to give heed to
- 9. D11:8: **keep:** (H8104) *(all of God's commandments) to guard, to watch, to protect, to give heed to:*
  - a. Why? D11:8 …**that ye may be strong,** *(prevail)* **and go in and possess** *(take ownership of)* **the land**…
- 10. D11:16: **take heed:** (H8104) - keep – (to yourselves) to guard, to watch, to protect, to give heed to
  - a. Why? …**that your heart be not deceived, and ye turn aside… and serve other gods…**
- 11. D11:32: **observe:** (H8104) …**to do all the statutes** *(ordinances)* **and judgments** *(litigation)*…

You will notice I have marked 5 uses of the same word used in the 6 verses that are similar in meaning.

I would conclude that this word is very important to understand as our main concept God is instructing us in.

So, a quick list of the detailed list above from Deuteronomy.

- **Respect** *(2 times: 10:12, 20)*
- **Walk** *(1 time: 10:12)*
- **Love** *(2 times: 10:13, 11)*
- **Serve** *(3 times: 10:12, 20, 11:16)*
- **Keep** *(5 times: 10:13, 11:1, 8, 16, 32)*
- **Cleave** *(1 time: 10:20)*
- **Swear** – as an oath to be loyal *(1 time: 10:20)*

These are seven concepts that God wants from us as His children, so He can provide for us in all categories of life. It has always been this way from the beginning.

When you read Deuteronomy 10ff you will notice that chapter 11 starts with the word "Therefore," and tells me that the chapter heading is wrong.

> *In the original and available texts, there are no capitals, periods, commas, chapter headings, no spaces between words. These are all added by the translators, so it might be easier to read in the language they are translating into. And many times, the translators will add punctuation and words to support their theology. But these additions can be discovered by the knowledge of "repetitions," the grammar*

and syntax of other words in the phrase/sentence/context, and by studies of key words and how they are used in other places.

Chapter 11 not only continues the discourse from chapter 10, chapter 11 concludes all the conditions mentioned in chapter 10 that God gave to His people to keep walking in His Word. Chapter 11 gives more instructions to keep His Word along with the blessings they will receive for being obedient. In this section, God promises that He will do what is needed for the land, so they can grow their crops, and feed their animals, just as He did in Egypt (chapter 10). That is, God will make sure His people will have enough food for all.

Just an observation, but when we as believers are in harmony living God's Word, God will cause the natural world around us to give us what we need so our land can also bless us. This is not only a promise to God's people in the past as a matter of record, but the principle that God will cause the Earth to respond favorably to us as we are faithful and honestly living His Word in our daily lives is still an ongoing promise for all believers, in any era. The following verses serve as a warning from God not to serve other gods or to worship them.

> **Deuteronomy 11:16-17 KJV**
> **16 Take heed to yourselves, that your heart be not deceived, and ye turn aside,**

and serve other gods, and worship them;

17 And *then* the LORD'S wrath be kindled against you, and he shut up the heaven, that there be no rain, and that the land yield not her fruit; and *lest* ye perish quickly from off the good land which the LORD giveth you.

In Deuteronomy 11:18-22 God gives specific things the families are to do so they can teach and remind themselves of the promises that God has made to them. This would be how they can carry out **"taking heed to yourselves"** in Deuteronomy 11:16 above. As you read the instructions on how the family is to keep God's Word in the forefront of their minds, you will notice a few local customs mentioned. Here is a list of what they were told to do.

1. V18a: **"... lay up these my words in your heart and in your soul, ..."** *or remember God's Word in your mind and lifestyle.*
2. V18b: **"... bind them for a sign upon your hand, that they may be as frontlets between your eyes"** *or write them on your palms so they will be always in front of you.*
3. V19: **"... teach them to your children, speaking of them when thou sittest in thine house, and when thou walkest by the way, when thou liest down, and when thou risest**

up." *Or teach them in your house, out on a walk, when you put them to sleep, when they wake up.*
4. **V20a: "... write them upon the door posts of thine house,"** *Just what is says, when they enter their house, they see God's Word. Maybe a psalm or similar short verse of encouragement.*
5. **V20b: "... and write them upon thy gates:"** *When they entered their house gate, they see God's Word, maybe a promise or short verse of encouragement.*

Then in Deuteronomy 11:21, 23-25 are more great promises to His people who will be living in the new land. These promises are in connection with a person or family who take an active role in renewing their thoughts to remember and live God's Word. God's principles are being applied in their lives, they are actively trying to live God's Word every day. As you can see, God gives us some things we can do to live His Word. This then brings us into what Paul refers to as the "renewed mind." Therefore, I will head in that direction also in this chapter in a moment. Since our goal is to live God's Word in our lives also. The promises God made to His people, if they will apply them *(to renew their mind)* will come to pass for them. His Word living in their lives!

Deuteronomy 11:21 KJV
21 That your days may be multiplied, and the days of your children, in the

land which the LORD sware unto your fathers to give them, as the days of heaven upon the earth.

Deuteronomy 11:23-25 KJV
23 Then will the LORD drive out all these nations from before you, and ye shall possess greater nations and mightier than yourselves.
24 Every place whereon the soles of your feet shall tread shall be yours: from the wilderness and Lebanon, from the river, the river Euphrates, even unto the uttermost sea shall your coast be.
25 There shall no man be able to stand before you: *for* the LORD your God shall lay the fear of you and the dread of you upon all the land that ye shall tread upon, as he hath said unto you.

CATEGORIES:
- V14-15: God will **provide food** for His people and their animals.
- V21: They will **live longer**.
- V23: God shall **drive out other nations** from their land, and they shall conquer countries and own their land even if they have a stronger military.
- V24: They can **claim the land as theirs** to possess as God has promised them to have.

- **V25: Other nations will not be able to stand against them**, they will be afraid of them because they see how their God protects them.

Look at these great promises how God will give everything they need to be healthy, live a long life, and have a strong military force, when they love God and keep His Word and apply it daily by renewing their minds. God had given them a choice, and God has given us the same choice also; it is by our freedom of will. No one is forcing you to live by the ethics of God's Word. No one is changing your mind for you, including God. That is all on your shoulders to change your attitudes and actions to apply God's Word.

His promises are eternal, and we can get the same results as promised in this record by applying the same principles in our lives. From the beginning God has always had the same stipulations to receive His promises that will bless us in all categories of life when we live His Word with the heart of love, not only *in the letter of God's Word*, **BUT ALSO IN *THE SPIRIT OF GOD'S WORD*.**

The opening of The Sermon on the Mount has the heart of a believer under the Law, but still applies today to receive the blessings from God. These are called by many, the "Beatitudes." These are moral attitudes, that is, issues of the heart, of decency and that which is right in a moral way within yourself and towards others. You will notice each Beatitude starts with the word "Blessed" and then mentions one moral quality and the result of applying that quality in your life. This repetition at the beginning of each Beatitude is a type of figure of speech that brings our attention that we will be "blessed" or have an inside joy from God's blessings on us as we have these qualities in our lives.

Matthew 5:2-12 KJV
2 And he opened his mouth, and taught them, saying,
3 Blessed *are* **the poor in spirit: for theirs is the kingdom of heaven.**
4 Blessed *are* **they that mourn: for they shall be comforted.**
5 Blessed *are* **the meek: for they shall inherit the earth.**
6 Blessed *are* **they which do hunger and thirst after righteousness: for they shall be filled.**
7 Blessed *are* **the merciful: for they shall obtain mercy.**
8 Blessed *are* **the pure in heart: for they shall see God.**
9 Blessed *are* **the peacemakers: for they shall be called the children of God.**
10 Blessed *are* **they which are persecuted for righteousness' sake: for theirs is the kingdom of heaven.**

11 Blessed are ye, when *men* shall revile you, and persecute *you,* and shall say all manner of evil against you falsely, for my sake.

12 Rejoice, and be exceeding glad: for great *is* your reward in heaven: for so persecuted they the prophets which were before you.

God has set before us a choice to live His Word with a right heart and soul, so we can receive His blessings, or to decide that His Word is not for us and receive the cursing of disobedience. This choice has never changed from the beginning regardless of what day and time we live in, whether under the Law, or under Grace.

> **Deuteronomy 11:26-28 KJV**
> **26 Behold, I set before you this day a blessing and a curse;** *(two choices, you must choose only one with any situation)*
> **27 A blessing, if ye obey** *(one choice)* **the commandments of the LORD your God**, which I command you this day:
> **28 And a curse, if ye will not obey** *(the other choice)* **the commandments of the LORD your God**, but turn aside out of the way which I command you this day, to go after other gods, which ye have not known.

> **Jeremiah 7:23 KJV**
> 23 But this thing commanded I them, saying, Obey my voice, and I will be your God, and ye shall be my people: and walk ye in all the ways that I have commanded you, that it may be well unto you.

The next relevant verse with the phrase "from the beginning" is in Psalm 119:160, and verifies that God's Word is from the beginning, and is true and that His judgments are righteous forever. So, His promises which are a part of His Word are also true and righteous by genuine logic. And His principles of learning and applying His Word are also true in all day and times, yes, including our day and time.

> **Psalms 119:160 KJV**
> 160 Thy word *is* true *from* the beginning: and every one of thy righteous judgments *endureth* for ever.

What are some of the parallel guidelines in the New Testament that we have read in the Old Testament in Deuteronomy 11:18-20 above? You will see that serving God with a pure heart was always what God wanted, and the way to that was to learn God's Word and then change your mind *(thoughts)* to live God's Word. That principle has not changed from the beginning.

God is *not* asking you to live a perfect life, but to honestly undertake renewing your thoughts to have the right attitude and motivation and love for God the best you can daily. Only Jesus Christ lived a perfect life without disobedience, so you could be forgiven for any past and future disobedience. That allows you to do the best you can when you are renewing your thoughts to do the right thing and to live righteously by applying God's Word.

> **Hebrews 8:10 KJV**
> **10 For this *is* the covenant that I will make with the house of Israel after those days, saith the Lord; <u>I will put my laws into their mind, and write them in their hearts</u>: and I will be to them a God, and they shall be to me a people:**

How will God do that? By the person's freedom of will to renew *(change)* their thoughts to apply God's Word. This is one level of understanding; another level - from the context - is that after the return of Christ, which as several stages, God will give us new knowledge, and we will not need to renew our minds as before. This is true for Israel and other believers in the Old Testament and the believers that were born-again after the Day of Pentecost.

> **Acts 20:19 KJV**

19 Serving the Lord with all humility of mind, ...

Mark 12:30-31 KJV
30 And thou shalt love the Lord thy God with all thy heart, and with all thy soul, and with all thy mind, and with all thy strength: this *is* the first commandment. 31 And the second *is* like, *namely* this, Thou shalt love thy neighbour as thyself. There is none other commandment greater than these.

Do those commandments in Acts 20:19 and Mark 12:30-31 sound familiar as being from Deuteronomy 10:12-11:28? What Acts 20:19 and Mark 12:30-31 summarize, Deuteronomy 10:12-11:28 give us the detail.

Romans 12:2 KJV
2 And be not conformed to this world: but be ye transformed by the renewing of your mind, that ye may prove what *is* that good, and acceptable, and perfect, will of God.

This is a choice *(via a command)* to the believers to make a conscious decision to *not* be conformed to the world, *but* to be transformed *(in their thoughts)* to live God's Word so they can prove God's Word to be good, acceptable, and perfect. How do they do that?

Well, Deuteronomy 11:18-20 gives a few principles of learning that can be applied to help with changing your thoughts in any day and time to live God's Word.

There are many verses on the topic of the renewed mind in Paul's epistles. Ephesians chapters 4-6 is a section which offers instructions about *how* to walk in accordance with God's Word in light of the mystery of Christ-in-you. Here are a few examples from Ephesians 4.

> **Ephesians 4:23-32 KJV**
> **23 And be renewed in the spirit of your mind;**
> **24 And that ye <u>put on the new man</u>, which after God is created in righteousness and true holiness.** *(Put on what God gave you in Christ, holy spirit)*
> **25 Wherefore putting away lying, speak every man truth with his neighbour: for we are members one of another.**
> **26 Be ye angry, and sin not: let not the sun go down upon your wrath:**
> **27 Neither give place to the devil.**
> **28 Let him that stole steal no more: but rather let him labour, working with *his* hands the thing which is good, that he may have to give to him that needeth.**
> **29 Let no corrupt communication proceed out of your mouth, but that**

which is good to the use of edifying, that it may minister grace unto the hearers.

30 And grieve not the holy Spirit of God, whereby ye are sealed unto the day of redemption. *(to grieve or make sorrowful our holy spirit is to NOT utilize the 9 manifestations you have to activate God's power in your life)*

31 Let all bitterness, and wrath, and anger, and clamour, and evil speaking, be put away from you, with all malice:

32 And be ye kind one to another, tenderhearted, forgiving one another, even as God for Christ's sake hath forgiven you.

All these verses show us that we are to change what we think so we can live God's Word. These verses tell us how to do it, that is, how to teach our mind to change. They tell you **"what not to do,"** and **"what to do"** in place of it. Deuteronomy 11:18-20 also gives us "how" to put God's Word in front of us so we can remember His Word. Here are the areas listed above in Ephesians that we need to change in our life, *(if relevant)*. The structure will be: The number equals *what* we change, the second tier *(small letter)* equals *how* to change. The first on the list is the general principle, then the following list are specific areas of change. This is part of putting on the new man;

Christ-in-you, some very practical steps we can all take and benefit from.

1) 4:23: *Be renewed in the spirit (heart) of your mind (thoughts)*
    a) 4:24: *Put on the new man (Christ-in-you)*
2) 4:25a: **Put away lying**
    a) 4:25b: Speak everyman the truth
3) 4:26a: **Be angry, and sin not**
    a) 4:26b: let not the sun go down upon your wrath *(resolve your anger with the other person before you go to bed. Not doing this is the sin in 4:26a)*
    b) 4:27: Neither give place to the devil. *(This is part of being angry and resolving it the same day. If you don't, that will give a way for the devil to provoke anger and hate towards the other person).*
4) 4:28a: **Let him that stole, steal no more**
    a) 4:28b: but rather let labour, working with his hands *(i.e., work for your things)*
    b) 4:28c: Work so you can also give to those with needs.

So, you change for two things, to supply your own needs and to help supply the needs of others.

5) 4:29a: **Let no corrupt communication come out your mouth**

a) But speak things that are good for edifying and ministering grace to the hearers.

Then, verses Ephesians 4:31-32 reiterates what we need to change, but Ephesians 4:30 reminds us to keep the operation of our gift holy spirit active which will be needed as we change our thinking with its associated actions.

   6) 4:30: **And grieve not the holy Spirit of God**, whereby ye are sealed unto the day of redemption.
      a) reminds us to keep the operation of our gift holy spirit active.
   7) 4:31: **Let all bitterness, and wrath, and anger, and clamour, and evil speaking**, be put away from you, *(along)* with all malice:
      a) 4:32: And be ye kind one to another, tenderhearted, forgiving one another, even as God for Christ's sake hath forgiven you.

There are many other verses and sections that tell us not to go in the way of wicked, and many other places that tell us to keep God's commandments. This is the same as what the Old Testament says, just in another way. The New Testament gives us how we can change our mind in a more direct way from His Word considering we now have Christ-in-us and that demonstrating this gift holy spirit is a part of how we renew our mind *(thoughts)*. Here are the first

19 verses in Proverbs Chapter one, Proverbs 1:1-7 are setting up the whole book of Proverbs for the readers. Proverbs was used to teach children the ways of God and the ways of the wicked, along with the results of following each way. The book of Proverbs teaches practical ways to renew the mind, so that Israel could live God's Word in their daily lives in Old Testament culture. Proverbs also spells out *our* choice in very clear terms. Teach your children Proverbs, and they will have a good understanding of good moral judgement in their lives that is godly.

Proverbs 1:1-19 KJV
1 The proverbs of Solomon the son of David, king of Israel;
2 To know wisdom and instruction; to perceive the words of understanding;
3 To receive the instruction of wisdom, justice, and judgment, and equity;
4 To give subtilty to the simple, to the young man knowledge and discretion.
5 A wise *man* **will hear, and will increase learning; and a man of understanding shall attain unto wise counsels:**
6 To understand a proverb, and the interpretation; the words of the wise, and their dark sayings.

7 The fear of the LORD *is* the beginning of knowledge: *but* fools despise wisdom and instruction.

8 My son, hear the instruction of thy father, and forsake not the law of thy mother:

9 For they *shall be* an ornament of grace unto thy head, and chains about thy neck.

10 My son, if sinners entice thee, consent thou not.

11 If they say, Come with us, let us lay wait for blood, let us lurk privily for the innocent without cause:

12 Let us swallow them up alive as the grave; and whole, as those that go down into the pit:

13 We shall find all precious substance, we shall fill our houses with spoil:

14 Cast in thy lot among us; let us all have one purse:

15 My son, walk not thou in the way with them; refrain thy foot from their path:

16 For their feet run to evil, and make haste to shed blood.

17 Surely in vain the net is spread in the sight of any bird.

18 And they lay wait for their *own* blood; they lurk privily for their *own* lives.

19 So *are* the ways of every one that is greedy of gain; *which* taketh away the life of the owners thereof.

Notice Proverbs 1:8-19 is the first lesson on combating the wicked. It deals with conspiring with criminals or enemies to steal and murder from good people. It is encouraging you to *not* join them or befriend them. If you were a leader of a country and you did this, you would be committing treason! This is the first lesson David shares in the opening of Proverbs, and it is fascinating that this still applies in our day and time.

In the first use of the phrase **"from the beginning"** we see how God tells His people that He is looking after the land they will soon occupy all year round. And He gives them many promises for their land and for their community if they will take heed to His Word and apply it in their lives. The condition was that the people had to endeavor to keep God's Word in their thoughts and teach their children also. We found in our study a list of seven things we are to observe so God can bless us. We are not to wait around and beg or overly praise God, thinking God will bless us for our much praising. **NO!** We are to renew our thoughts to live His Word, and then God will bless us in our life. The seven things we are to observe as we renew our thoughts: This is the direction I will be taking with this book.

- Respect God
- Walk in His ways
- Love God
- Serve God
- Keep His Word
- Cleave unto His Word
- Swear – as an oath to be loyal to God

These have always been God's requirements for His people to do so that He could bless them from the beginning.

2: Paul's ministry: to teach "The fellowship of the mystery"

Ephesians 3:4-7 KJV
4 Whereby, when ye read, ye may understand my knowledge in the mystery of Christ)
5 Which in other ages was not made known unto the sons of men, as it is now revealed unto his holy apostles and prophets by the Spirit;
6 That the Gentiles should be fellowheirs, and of the same body, and partakers of his promise in Christ by the gospel:
7 Whereof I was made a minister, according to the gift of the grace of God given unto me by the effectual working of his power.

Ephesians 3:9 KJV
9 And to make all *men* see what *is* the fellowship of the mystery, which from the beginning of the world hath been hid in God, ~~who created all things by Jesus Christ:~~ *(not in the majority of major Greek texts, added by many translators to support their denomination's theology).*

Ephesians is the greatest revelation to the church in the sense that the first three chapters explain what God has done for all mankind in His son Jesus Christ, to the end that all of mankind can have fellowship *(a relationship)* with God. Through God's mercy, Jesus Christ was sent to repair the broken fellowship *(relationship)* and to give access to God for all of mankind for those that believe. The gift holy of spirit that was given on the Day of Pentecost is by the means by which God gave us a way to have a relationship with Him through His son's accomplishments.

Through what Jesus Christ did, *(it is no longer just Israel that are God's chosen, but all of mankind regardless of their blood line)*, all nations have the same promise from God to be partakers of this great mystery that has been hidden in God, from the beginning. The mystery that they are all a part of the same body, and the same hope of eternal life with the same spiritual body Jesus Christ has now. We had nothing to do with this action from God, and God only requires you to "believe" so you can receive His gift holy spirit.

This is salvation, and salvation is not the end of being a Christian. Salvation gives you the spiritual ability you will need to defeat Satan, God's arch enemy. But, *you* will have to discipline your mind *(thoughts and actions)* by changing how you live, and by learning how to live God's Word to access this spiritual power in your life, and the people you may minister to. God is not going change your thoughts for you. The renewed mind is something you do by your freedom of will and is voluntary. God has set up your brain to destroy habits you are replacing with the new habits to live God's Word. This is how metamorphosis works in your brain. You don't control the internal process, but you control the habits you want to change and when you want to change them. How your brain destroys the old habits and replaces them is not your responsibility. God set up your brain to naturally take care of it automatically, by what many call "an internal involuntary action." Like how your heart beats 60-70 times a minute, and you don't control it at all, it just beats on its own automatically. The brain works the same way, as *you change* your old habit to the new and improved habit, the brain literally *destroys* the old habit and *replaces* it with your new and improved habit. This is the metamorphosis that takes place inside your brain. The only thing left is your memory of the old habit, it physically no longer exists, literally!

I bring this up now because Ephesians has two main sections, a doctrinal side *(Ephesians 1-3)* and a practical side *(Ephesians 4-6:20)* After you are born-again, by receiving the gift of holy spirit, there is much work to be done on your part to fully access the relationship *(fellowship)* you now have with God and His son Jesus Christ. You are in a relationship, but until you start interacting with God through Jesus Christ via your gift of holy spirit and with your habits to live God's Word, your relationship will lack depth and closeness. As with any new relationship, you want to learn about them, and endeavour to change some of your habits to bless them and show them you care about them. It takes a conscious effort on your part to learn how to love them and build a close-knit relationship with them.

Having a new relationship requires work to keep it vital and productive. Merely *thinking* about the relationship and where it might go is *not* going to change anything or make it more vital and productive. The same is true with our new relationship with God. God is not going change your habits or thoughts to build the relationship for you. But God has given you His Word so *you can change* what you think by "putting on" His Word in a practical way. The gift of holy spirit is not going to change *(or take away)* your habits to live God's Word on its own, without your guidance.[6] The gift of holy

---

[6] John 16:13 KJV
13 Howbeit when he *(it)*, the Spirit of truth, is come, he *(it)* will guide you into all truth: <u>for he *(it)* shall not speak *(act)* of himself *(itself)*</u>; but whatsoever he *(it)* shall hear, *that* shall he *(it)* speak: and he *(it)* will shew you things to come. *Your gift will not act on its own but will act on God's instructions as you decide to activate the gift holy spirit.* 1 Corinthians 14:32 KJV: And the spirits of the prophets are subject to the prophets. Also, Arbib, Peter., "Can I Really Speak in Tongues?" ref to "he" = "it" p. 139-141.

spirit will not take away your bad habits because that is *your* responsibility via the principles of the renewed mind taught by Paul to the Church. If God, or the gift of holy spirit did change your bad habits without your assistance, then that would be outside of your freedom of will, *(or by possession.)* But it is also outside of God's ability to help you, because God does not and will not ever possess you ever! God can and does give you revelation at times when you least expect it, but, *if you* have already been praying about the situation, and/or thinking about what you could do, God is answering your concern.

God knows your heart and will give you what you need for the situation you are already actively thinking about and/or praying about. Here is another verse which teaches the gift of holy spirit is subordinate to you. This is an important truth because it teaches you that *you* are in control of your spirit, you decide when to operate any of the nine manifestations.

> **1 Corinthians 14:32 KJV**
> **32 And the spirits of the prophets are subject** *(subordinate, put into subjection)* [7] **to the prophets.**

---

[7] Thayer, Joseph H., *(Thayer's Greek-English Lexicon of the New Testament)*, Baker Books House, Grand Michigan, 24th printing. p. 645, ref: 5293

Therefore *(because God or His gift holy spirit cannot change or take away your bad habits for you)* Paul wrote by revelation, Ephesians 4:1-6:20 to teach you how to build your relationship with God and His son Jesus Christ. There are two areas you need to build-up, so you can build-up your relationship; your mind, and your gift holy spirit.[8] This chapter will concentrate on building up your mind, your thoughts, your habits that are all in the physical realm, as Ephesians 4:1 6:20 teaches us. Where you interact *(in the physical realm)* with other believers as you still live in this world. It is essential to build and keep a tight body of believers to carry out the work of the ministry, as Paul teaches while awaiting the return of Christ.[9]

Chapter 4 starts off with Paul exhorting the believers to walk *(to conduct their life)* worthy *(suitable)* of their calling from God with modesty, meekness, forbearance, and endurance, with God's love, endeavouring to keep the unity of the spirit bonded together in peace. This is all done by our freedom of will to act in these ways, and part of our actions will

---

[8] Arbib, Peter., *(20+ Benefits Speaking in Tongues Has for You)*, Sound Wisdom Publications, Mooresville, IN. 2018. Chapter 3, "Speaking in Tongues Edifies You, It Builds You Up.

[9] Philippians 1:23-25 KJV
23 For I am in a strait betwixt two, having a desire to depart, and to be with Christ; which is far better:
24 **Nevertheless to abide in the flesh** is **more needful for you**.
25 And having this confidence, I know that I shall abide and continue with you all for your furtherance and joy of faith;

be utilizing our gift holy spirit by our freedom of will also, so we will see some of the fruit of the spirit that is listed verse 4:2.

> **Ephesians 4:1-3 KJV**
> **1 I therefore, the prisoner of the Lord, beseech you that <u>ye walk worthy of the vocation wherewith ye are called,</u>**
> **2 With all lowliness and meekness, with longsuffering, forbearing one another in love;**
> **3 Endeavouring to keep the unity of the Spirit in the bond of peace.**

If Paul exhorts us... then he is *asking* us in a strong manor to change our habits and to do something that will benefit us.

> *If God is asking us by Paul's revelation to the Ephesians to conduct ourselves suitable to our calling from God, then this will be by <u>our</u> freedom of will to change, right? Is this suggesting that God, or the gift of holy spirit will control our mind and change our habits for us? No!*

Paul *(or God by Paul's revelation to the Ephesians)* is instructing us on what is required to change our own habits *(formed from thoughts)*, so we can live *in* God's Word, and live *in* fellowship *(a relationship)* with Him. The first thing Paul instructs us on is the seven doctrines *(or tenets)* of Christianity, that is, the seven standards that original Christianity is based on.[10] Most of these were also original standards for the Law Administration. Ephesians 4:4-6

1. ONE body
2. ONE spirit
3. ONE hope
4. ONE Lord
5. ONE faith
6. ONE baptism
7. ONE God

Why do you think that these seven **"ones"** were the first things mentioned in the beginning of *the renewed mind section* of Ephesians?

Because Ephesus, along with other Greek cities, worshiped more than **one** God, and had many beliefs along with many spirits, <u>and</u> many lords, <u>and</u> many hopes, <u>and</u> many faiths, <u>and</u>[11] many baptisms, etc. Paul had to teach these seven **"one"** tenets of Christianity to the believers. These multiple god doctrines along with other multiple religious beliefs was a deep-rooted part of the philosophy in Greek culture and was even looked upon as a highly

---

[10] Nessle, Jon O., *(The 7 Ones of Original Christianity Syllabus)*, Next Reformation Publishing Co. Plainfield, IN. 2018

[11] I have purposely used the figure of speech "Polysyndeton" *(many ands)* to place emphasis on "each" of the things listed… This is a contrast of the "ones" list Paul brings our attention to. One vs Many.

educated status symbol to have such worldly knowledge. The road leading to Ephesus and the roads in Ephesus were lined with all the many gods that were worshipped from all the Greek cities. Ephesus was also the largest port city for trade, it was a very influential city with great political and religious power.

Polytheism *(worshipping many gods)* was the largest issue Paul had to deal with among the Gentiles, to whom he was called to minister. What was the very first written commandment to Moses from the beginning? In Deuteronomy is the first commandment that has carried through in all administrations even to this day and time.

> **Deuteronomy 6:4-5 KJV**
> **4** Hear, O Israel: The LORD our God *is* one LORD:
> **5** And thou shalt love the LORD thy God with all thine heart, and with all thy soul, and with all thy might.
>
> **Exodus 20:2-3 KJV**
> **2** I *am* the LORD thy God, which have brought thee out of the land of Egypt, out of the house of bondage.
> **3** Thou shalt have no other gods before me.
> **Mark 12:28-29 KJV**

28 And one of the scribes came, and having heard them reasoning together, and perceiving that he had answered them well, asked him, Which is the first commandment of all?

29 And Jesus answered him, The first of all the commandments *is*, Hear, O Israel; The Lord our God is one Lord:

Here is a photograph of the entrance to Ephesus showing all the pedestals that used to have all the statues of each god as you entered the city.

Entrance to Ephesus.

---

[12] Aykin, Nuray, (*Pomegranates and Grapes*), iUniverse, 2012, Photo Credit via Thinkstock

With the aim of having fellowship *(a relationship)* with the one true God, the believers in Ephesus had to get rid of all their thinking and multi-god rituals about all the other gods, lords, beliefs, hopes, baptisms, faiths, etc. They needed to *replace* those ideas and doctrines with the "**one**" doctrine from the "**one**" true God in their minds by changing their old beliefs with new beliefs that line up with the "**one**" true God's written Word that has not changed since the beginning. This was the very first thing they had to change before they could even think about having fellowship *(a relationship)* with God and His son Jesus Christ.

Then Ephesians 4:8-10 teaches us that Jesus Christ defeated all the gods, all the faiths, all the lords, all the beliefs, all the hopes, all the baptisms, all the spirits that these people were worshiping and serving in their daily lives.

> **Ephesians 4:8-10 KJV**
> **8 Wherefore he saith, When he ascended up on high, he led captivity captive, and gave gifts unto men.
> 9 (Now that he ascended, what is it but that he also descended first into the lower parts of the earth?
> 10 He that descended is the same also that ascended up far above all heavens, that he might fill all things.)**

If I were worshipping many gods, and Paul visited my city and preached Jesus Christ, along with healing many people and he also taught that Jesus Christ defeated all the gods in my city to show that there is **"one"** true God, and now I believed also. I would want to know what I need to believe to worship and serve the **"one"** true God. Ephesians 4:11-12 tells us what God has given to the church via His gift ministries to men and women to help us change our old habits and ways, and to help us put on the true Word of God, not just the written Word. But also, as taught by our ministers who receive revelation to guide the local believers.

> **Ephesians 4:11-12 KJV**
> **11 And he gave some, apostles; and some, prophets; and some, evangelists; and some, pastors and teachers;**
> **12 For the perfecting of the saints, for the work of the ministry, for the edifying of the body of Christ:**

Then, in Ephesians 4:15-16 we see the first thing Paul mentions from the **"one"** list is **"the one body."** How important is that to understand in the context of living the mystery, being fellowheirs and of the same body? That is: living in "the fellowship of the mystery," the body of Christ *(Christ-in-you)* that is all about understanding the mystery that Paul revealed in Ephesians and other epistles.

We must understand that we are all part of *"one body"* and because of what Jesus Christ did for all of mankind, we now have the *"one"* gift holy spirit that gives us a common bond with all the other believers. We are all a part of the *"one"* spirit that God has given every born-again believer. That's why it is *"one"* body in Christ! That is why we are fellowheirs with each other. We are also a part of the ONE hope of the return of Christ and eternal life with God and His son Jesus Christ.

> Ephesians 4:15-16 KJV
> 15 But speaking the truth in love, may grow up into him in all things, which is the head, *even* Christ:
> 16 From whom the whole body fitly joined together and compacted by that which every joint supplieth, according to the effectual working in the measure of every part, maketh increase of the body unto the edifying of itself in love.
>
> Ephesians 3:3-6 KJV
> 3 How that by revelation he made known unto me the mystery; (as I wrote afore in few words,
> 4 Whereby, when ye read, ye may understand my knowledge in the mystery of Christ)
> 5 Which in other ages was not made known unto the sons of men, as it is

now revealed unto his holy apostles and prophets by the Spirit;
6 That the Gentiles should be ==fellowheirs, and of the same body==, and partakers of his promise in Christ by the gospel:

Ephesians 1:22-23 KJV
22 And hath put all *things* under his feet, and gave him *to be* the head over all *things* to the church,
23 ==Which is his body==, the fulness of him that filleth all in all.

Ephesians 2:16 KJV
16 And that he might reconcile both unto God ==in one body== by the cross, having slain the enmity thereby:

The first thing we need to understand so we can have fellowship *(a relationship)* with God and His son Jesus Christ is that we are an important part of the *"one"* body, we all have a common bond with the *"one"* God and Father. We need to understand that we are *"one"* family of faith, because of the *"one"* gift of holy spirit that we all have in common.

When we start thinking in these *"one"* terms, we will start to look at other Christians as part of God's family spiritually, and not look down upon them because they don't believe exactly like ourselves.

This can happen because God's arch enemy Satan has caused all kinds of small errors in the original Christian doctrine, in the "7 *"ones"* above. Various errors in Christian doctrines deny the gift of holy spirit completely or introduce just enough error in how it is operated, so that believers can't defeat Satan in their lives. No one ministry has "all the answers," we all a part of the *"one"* body, regardless of the right and wrong doctrines we all have. As we apply what works from God's Word with our renewed mind, we are all contributing to that *"one"* body, and it will grow in God's love.[13] We need to promote what we agree on, to endeavour to keep *(or guard)* the unity of the peace in the *"one"* body. He is a list of seven attitudes that mimic the seven of the nine fruits of the spirit.

> **Ephesians 4:2-4 KJV**
> 2 With all lowliness and meekness, with longsuffering, forbearing one another in love;
> 3 Endeavouring to keep the unity of the Spirit in the bond of peace.
> 4 *There is* one body, and one Spirit, even as ye are called in one hope of your calling;

---

[13] Ephesians 4:16 KJV
16 From whom the whole body fitly joined together and compacted by that which every joint supplieth, according to the effectual working in the measure of every part, maketh increase of the body unto the edifying of itself in love.

For all Christians to see the greatness of the *"one"* body, we are going to have to realize we will meet other Christians that are living the Word the best they can with what they have been taught, whether it is a small amount of truth, or a large amount of truth. Instead of always confronting them with the error you notice, find the good they have in the areas they are living God's Word that you can agree on, and bless them for their contribution to the *"one"* body.

Then in Ephesians 4:17-32 Paul shares how the believers need to change their different old habits by replacing them with new habits that will not only promote the *"7 ones"* of Christianity in their physical walk, but also promote the unity of the family of faith in the *"one" body* collectively in God's Word. These are all in areas that God requires *you* to take an active role in changing your thoughts with the accompanied actions of the old habit. Ephesians 4:17-19 is where the believers are before they change their old habits, and he admonishes them not to walk *(live)* in the vanity of their understanding.

> **Ephesians 4:17-19 KJV**
> **17 This I say therefore, and testify in the Lord, that ye henceforth walk not as other Gentiles walk, in the vanity of their mind,**
> **18 Having the understanding darkened,**

being alienated from the life of God through the ignorance that is in them, because of the blindness of their heart: 19 Who being past feeling have given themselves over unto lasciviousness, to work all uncleanness with greediness.

If Paul is admonishing them not to live by their vain understanding because of what they have been taught and lived, then who is supposed to change their thinking and lifestyle? If someone admonishes me not to something, am I not responsible to act on that guidance and am I not responsible to change my mind? Isn't that assumed? *(Yes)*. It is no different here in Ephesians, Paul is giving guidance to the new believers to *not* live like other Gentiles, with a list of things not to do.

Paul taught them the truths in Christ and *that they put on* what God has created in them, the gift of holy spirit, Christ-in-you. He made sure they understood that *they* were the ones who changes their own mind *(understanding)*. And *that they most put off* the old habits which are corrupt in nature.

> **Ephesians 4:24 KJV**
> 24 And that ye put on the new man, which after God is created in righteousness and true holiness.
> **Ephesians 4:22 KJV**

22 That ye put off concerning the former conversation the old man, which is corrupt according to the deceitful lusts;

Who changes your old habits? Who changes your wrong thinking? Does God? Does the gift of holy spirit? Do you see the word I underlined in the above two verses? **"Ye" is the translation for the word "you" in old English.** Yes, *you* utilize God's Word, and *you* are the one who actively changes your old habit to a new habit by replacing your actions to do the new habit, and *not* to do the old habit. Yes, *you* can operate the gift of holy spirit as *you* change your actions, and *you* are the one that must *not* do the old habit anymore. **God or the gift of holy spirit will not take away the old habit, that is your job!**

Then the balance of Ephesians 4:25-32 are direct actions that each believer can do with their actions to change the old habits with the replacement of the new habits. And remember that the *"7 ones"* of Christianity are overshadowing this whole chapter. This is the first chapter in second section of Ephesians that starts to teach what we need to *put on and live* God's Word.

Ephesians 4:25 KJV
25 Wherefore putting away lying, speak every man truth with his neighbour: for

we are members one of another. *(Stop lying >>> speak the truth. There are 2 layers here.... One layer: Speak God's Word. The second layer: Speak truthfully when taking with another person with any subject)*

Ephesians 4:26 KJV
26 Be ye angry, and sin not: let not the sun go down upon your wrath: *(Don't go to bed angry, >>> resolve it first)*

Ephesians 4:28 KJV
28 Let him that stole steal no more: but rather let him labour, working with *his* hands the thing which is good, that he may have to give to him that needeth. *(Don't steal anymore >>> Work an honest job so your need is taken care of AND you can help others in need with your extra abundance)*

Ephesians 4:29 KJV
29 Let no corrupt communication proceed out of your mouth, but that which is good to the use of edifying, that it may minister grace unto the hearers. *(Don't speak words that hurt others >>> Speak words that build them up, so the words minister favor to them)*

Ephesians 4:31-32 KJV

31 Let all bitterness, and wrath, and anger, and clamour, and evil speaking, be put away from you, with all malice: 32 And be ye kind one to another, tenderhearted, forgiving one another, even as God for Christ's sake hath forgiven you.

If you want to find one of the themes in any book or chapter, you will need find a word of phrase that is used *more* times in the book or chapter you are studying. It may or may not be a part of a figure of speech related to "repetition," but nevertheless, because the word or phrase is used more in any other book in the Bible, it is still showing you a major theme that the book is bringing to your attention.

The word I am referring to is the word **"walk"** and its various translations from the same Greek word. The word **"walk"** is used eight times in the book of Ephesians, and eight times in the book of Acts, more than any other books in the epistles. The book of Acts is the rise and expansion of the first century Church which shows the new Christian believers learning *how* to walk as a Christian. And the epistle to the Ephesians is where the older, mature walk of a Christian believer is exemplified. We will look at the uses in Ephesians. Two times in the doctrinal section *(Ephesians 1-3)* and six times in the practical application section *(Ephesians 4:1-6:20)*.

The two times that **"walk"** appears in the doctrinal section are in Ephesians 2:2 and 2:10. The first one is about your past; the second is about your future.

> **Ephesians 2:2 KJV** *(past)*
> 2 Wherein in time past ye walked according to the course of this world, according to the prince of the power of the air, the spirit that now worketh in the children of disobedience:
>
> **Ephesians 2:10 KJV** *(future)*
> 10 For we are his workmanship, created in Christ Jesus unto good works, which God hath before ordained that we should walk in them.

The next six list the things we should walk in, or not walk in.

> **Ephesians 4:1 KJV**
> 1 I therefore, the prisoner of the Lord, beseech you that ye walk worthy of the vocation wherewith ye are called,
>
> **Ephesians 4:17 KJV**
> 17 This I say therefore, and testify in the Lord, that ye henceforth walk not as other Gentiles walk, in the vanity of their mind,

Ephesians 5:2 KJV
2 And walk in love, as Christ also hath loved us, and hath given himself for us an offering and a sacrifice to God for a sweetsmelling savour.

Ephesians 5:8 KJV
8 For ye were sometimes darkness, but now *are ye* light in the Lord: walk as children of light:

Ephesians 5:15 KJV
15 See then that ye walk circumspectly, not as fools, but as wise,

1) **A)** Ephesians 4:1: Walk worthy of your calling from God.
2) **B)** Ephesians 4:17: (2x) Don't walk in the vanity of your thoughts.
3) **C)** Ephesians 5:2: Walk in God's love.
4) **B)** Ephesians 5:8: Walk in God's light, as children of light.
5) **A)** Ephesians 5:15: Walk accurately, diligently, truthfully, according to God's Word.

You will notice that Ephesians 4:1-6:9 give very specific guidance on what we need to do to change our mental habits to line up with God's Word, that is, what we need to do to "walk" on the Word of God mentally. And if you look at the "A, B, and C" pairs, you will see this outline gives even more proof on how The Word cross-checks its intended interpretation!

Here is another contextual check that the intended interpretation is to be centered upon the renewed mind in practice. Ephesians 4:17 tells us not to walk in the vanity of our mind, and Ephesians 5:8 tells us to walk in God's light *(not our own light, which is darkness in God's Word - opposite of Ephesians 4:17)*. The verses between these two verses *("B" in the above structural outline)* tell us to "put off" the old man *(way)*, our vanity or our own light, and to be "renewed in the spirit *(heart)* of you mind" by "putting on" the new man *(way)*, God's way, or God's light, Ephesians 4:18-5:1. The more abridged verses that share the general truth without the specific details are Ephesians 4:20-24.

- **Outline "A"** has is a pair of verses with the word "walked" in them that "correspond" to each other: Eph. 4:1: Walk worthy: Eph. 5:15: Walk truthfully.
- **Outline "B"** has a pair of verses with the word "walked" in them that are "opposites" to each other: Eph. 4:17 Don't walk full in the vanity of your mind *(thoughts)*. Eph. 5:8 Walk in God's light.

- **Outline "C"** sits by itself, Eph. 5:2 Walk in God's Love. If you do **"A, and B"** you will be living **"C."**

It is interesting to note that after Ephesians 3:1ff explains the "fellowship of the mystery" that God hid from the beginning. Ephesians 4:1ff gives us what we need to do so we can live *(or walk)* in this "fellowship of the mystery." It does not emphasize "walking by the spirit" *(operating the nine manifestations)*, but it emphasizes "walking with a renewed mind," replacing our old habits or ways that are corrupt and against God, with new habits or ways that are based on the teachings of the mystery that was revealed to Paul by revelation. And this outline corroborates the practical application that is offered in chapters 4:1ff to 6:20 in Ephesians. It is another check and balance in this section of God's Word to make sure you rightly divide His word in this section.

The word "walk" in the Greek is the word "peripateō" (G4043) and is pronounced "*per-ee-pat-eh'-o*" and is the verb form and means: *From G4012 and G3961; to tread all around, that is, <u>walk</u> at large (especially as proof of ability); figuratively <u>to live, deport oneself, follow</u> (as a companion or votary): - go, be* *occupied with, walk (about).*[14] From Thayer's: *1) to walk, 1a) to make one's way, progress; to make due use of opportunities, 1b) Hebrew for, to live, 1b1) to regulate one's life, 1b2) to conduct one's self, 1b3) to pass one's life.*[15]

It is also interesting that Paul made sure the truth about the "one body" is the foundation of the "fellowship of the mystery" and that what we think and act on is what we need to work on in the physical realm. This theme continues in Ephesians 5:1 to 6:9 and then the context changes in Ephesians 6:10-18 to putting on the spiritual power that we have received in our gift of holy spirit, "walking by the spiritual power." To be fully clothed with God's Word *(in our thoughts)* and the power He has given us *(the nine manifestations of the gift of holy spirit)*, are the two areas we must attend to.

One area, which takes up Ephesians 3:1 to 6:9 *(4+ chapters)* is taking care of what we think and how we act as believers by replacing our old corrupt ways with new incorrupt ways of honesty and truth based on God's Word. This is done in the physical realm by our freedom of will.

---

[14] Strong, James. *(The New Strong's Exhaustive Concordance of the Bible)*, Thomas Nelson Publishers. 1996. *(Greek Dictionary)*, p. 70, ref: 4043

[15] Meyers, Rick, *(Thayer's Greek Lexicon Dictionary)* E-Sword Software Version 11.1.0, Copyright ©2000-2017. Ref: 4043

The second area, which is mentioned in Ephesians 6:10-18 *(9 verses)* instructs us to learn how to operate all nine manifestations, when you understand that this section is talking about "putting on the whole armour" which is mentioned in Ephesians 6:10-11, it is mainly about manifesting your gift of holy spirit. To "stand against the devil" you will need to operate the nine manifestations. That requires your believing to do it with boldness. You don't need to have a "perfectly" renewed mind to operate any of the nine manifestations, but you will need to believe you can operate them. This is also done by your freedom of will.

You may need some instruction, but once you understand how each manifestation is operated in a similar fashion, you should be able to operate any of them when needed. But in the full context of these nine verses, *(Ephesians 3:1 – 6:18)* it will be required of you to also equip you mind *(understanding)* with the teachings from God's Word. You will need to understand the mystery as Paul revealed it.[16] And you will need to renew the heart of your mind to live God's Word according to the "one body," so you can be fully clothed both in the physical realm *(your*

---

[16] Ephesians 3:3-4 KJV
3 How that by revelation he made known unto me the mystery; (as I wrote afore in few words,
4 Whereby, when ye read, ye may understand my knowledge in the mystery of Christ)

renewed mind) and in the spiritual realm *(your gift of holy spirit in operation)*. Notice in Ephesians 6:18 is talking about speaking in tongues to make supplication for all the saints, this is the last thing mentioned before the closing comments. It is perhaps one of greatest ways to stand against the devil you can do 24/7/365.

Ephesians 6:10-18 KJV
10 Finally, my brethren, be strong in the Lord, and in the power of his might.
11 Put on the whole armour of God, that ye may be able to stand against the wiles of the devil.
12 For we wrestle not against flesh and blood, but against principalities, against powers, against the rulers of the darkness of this world, against spiritual wickedness in high *places.*
13 Wherefore take unto you the whole armour of God, that ye may be able to withstand in the evil day, and having done all, to stand.
14 Stand therefore, having your loins girt about with truth, and having on the breastplate of righteousness;
15 And your feet shod with the preparation of the gospel of peace;
16 Above all, taking the shield of faith, wherewith ye shall be able to quench all the fiery darts of the wicked.

**17 And take the helmet of salvation, and the sword of the Spirit, which is the word of God:
18 Praying always with all prayer and supplication in the Spirit,** *(speaking in tongues)* **and watching thereunto with all perseverance and supplication for all saints;**

Ephesians 6:10-18 is the best summary of what we need to do in both the physical realm to be fully equipped with God's Word via the renewed mind, and in the spiritual realm by learning how to put on the whole armour of God, with all nine manifestations in operation in your life.

This is the *"how"* to live in "the fellowship of the mystery," in the "one body," being "fellowheirs and of the same body in Christ." This is the how-to instruction from God's Word to build your vital and personal relationship with God your Father and your Lord Jesus Christ. The epistle to the Ephesians shows us what it is like when believers believe the revelation from God via Paul about the one body, the mystery. Ephesians shows us how to have a vital and personal relationship with God by demonstrating God's power via operating the gift of holy spirit and by renewing our minds to live God's Word every day.

3: God's Choice and Our Choice

Blessing or Curse

God chose us from the beginning to be saved through believing the truth and being purified by the spirit. We have been given choices to make as well, and our choices have real consequences. Our proper response to God is twofold. First, we accept His son as our savior, and second, we realign our habits to live by the tenets of scripture. We are called to live in the one body and the one faith and according to the riches of the mystery, which is Christ-in-you. Making the right choices enable us to receive God's richest blessings in our lives.

> **Deuteronomy 11:26-28, KJV**
> **26 Behold, I set before you this day a blessing and a curse;**
> **27 A blessing, if ye obey the commandments of the LORD your God, which I command you this day:**
> **28 And a curse, if ye will not obey the commandments of the LORD your God, but turn aside out of the way which I command you this day, to go after other gods, which ye have not known.**

God provided a clear choice between a blessing and a curse. The curse would accompany the wrong choice; blessings result from the right choice. Real choice has existed from the beginning. Adam and Eve had a choice between two trees, the tree of life; God's knowledge, and the tree of the knowledge of good and evil; worldly knowledge. These two types of contrasting knowledge fit throughout the whole Bible within the renewed mind category. Tragically, they made the wrong choice, and the consequences have unfolded throughout human history ever since.

In the first use of the Greek word translated "choose" or "choice" we see a desire to choose for the Christ's return over teaching the believers because the return of Christ is preferred to live as a born-again Christian. In this study, we will study the Greek verb *hairēsomai (G138)* which occurs three times in the Greek New Testament and only in the middle voice.[17] The first use, *(specifically hairēsomai -- Future, Indicative, Middle)* is found in Philippians. The middle voice emphasizes the self-interest of the one preferring or deciding.

Philippians 1:16-26, KJV

---

[17] Zodhiates, Spiros, Th.D., *The Complete Word Study Dictionary: New Testament* AMG Publishers, Chattanooga, TN, Revised 1993, p.98, ref 138.

16 The one preach Christ of contention, not sincerely, supposing to add affliction to my bonds:
17 But the other of love, knowing that I am set for the defence of the gospel.
18 What then? notwithstanding, every way, whether in pretence, or in truth, Christ is preached; and I therein do rejoice, yea, and will rejoice.
19 For I know that this shall turn to my salvation through your prayer, and the supply of the Spirit of Jesus Christ,
20 According to my earnest expectation and my hope, that in nothing I shall be ashamed, but that with all boldness, as always, so now also Christ shall be magnified in my body, whether it be by life, or by death.
21 For me to live is Christ, and to die is gain.
22 But if I live in the flesh, this is the fruit of my labor: yet what I shall choose (hairēsomai G138) I wot not.
23 For I am in a strait betwixt two, having a desire to depart, and to be with Christ; which is far better:
24 Nevertheless to abide in the flesh is more needful for you.
25 And having this confidence, I know that I shall abide and continue with you all for your furtherance and joy of faith;

26 That your rejoicing may be more abundant in Jesus Christ for me by my coming to you again.

The specific Greek terminology paired with the contextual information shows us that Paul knew he had a choice regarding self-interest. He was honest about the fact that his personal preference was to enter the presence of the Lord Jesus Christ, but he also knew that the greater need was to choose to stay in the presence of those who needed his teaching ministry.

Clearly, Paul's personal preference was the return of Jesus Christ over preaching the Word, if he could make that choice. Certainly, it is a far better choice for all believers to receive their new bodies and finally be living with God and His son Jesus Christ. But Paul did not actually have that choice in real time. The Old English phrase "I wot not," as used here, basically means that the timing of the return of Christ is still a secret with God *(and that is true even unto this day)*. God is the only one who knows when He will send Jesus Christ to gather together all the believers *(the Old Testament believers and the New Testament believers in two separate gatherings)*, when

He will also change our bodies to be like Christ's body when he ascended to heaven.[18]

In the second usage we see God's choice for us to a member of His family. The second occurrence of *hairēsomai (G138)* is in 2nd Thessalonians 2, and we may consider this use to be our key verse to a greater understanding of the vivid reality of *choice*. This second use reveals that God's desire - His choice from the beginning - was to have us be a part of His family. That relationship is in His best self-interest. Of course, it is also in ours.

> **2 Thessalonians 2:13-15, KJV**
> **13 But we are bound to give thanks always to God for you, brethren beloved of the Lord, because God hath from the beginning chosen (*hairēsomai (G138)*) you to salvation through sanctification of the Spirit and belief of the truth:**
> **14. Whereunto he called you by our gospel, to the obtaining of the glory of our Lord Jesus Christ.**
> **15. Therefore, brethren, stand fast, and hold the traditions which ye have been taught, whether by word, or our epistle.**

---

[18] Phil 3:20-21

In this second use of the term, we see two components of Christian salvation: belief, and sanctification *(verse 13)*. In response to God choosing us, we believers should choose to live and regulate our own lives according to the standards of scripture, renewing our minds.

The word "called" in verse 14 is the word kaleó (G2564) and is pronounced "kal-eh'-o" and means: 1; *"to call to someone in order that he may come or go somewhere. 1D: In the sense of to invite: ... Metaphorically, to invite to anything, e.g. of Jesus to call (us) to repentance, exhort (Matt 9:13, implied in Mark 2:17). Of God, 1st Cor. 1:9; 2nd Thess. 2:14; 1st Tim. 6:12; 1st Peter 2:9, 5:10; Rev. 19:9."*[19]

Because God has *chosen* us and *called* us to Himself and to eventually obtain glory *(verse 14)*, Paul admonishes us to respond by standing fast and to holding firmly to the traditions we have been taught *(verse 15)*. It's a very real invitation, and our response determines the outcome.

The terms in verse 15 assist us to more clearly see what it takes to grow up in Christ and to mature as a Christian. First, we will take a brief look at **"standing**

---

[19] Zodhiates, Spiros, Th.D., (*The Complete Word Study Dictionary: New Testament)*, AMG Publishers, Chattanooga, TN, Revised 1993, pp. 811-812, ref: 2564, def: 1, and then 1D.

fast." "Fast" is not a reference to speed, but to firmness. Here is a list of five areas in which we are to stand fast along with the scripture reference.[20]

1. We are to **stand fast** *in the faith*. 1st Corinthians 16:13.
2. We are to **stand fast** *in the liberty*. Galatians 5:1.
3. We are to **stand fast** *in one spirit and one soul*. Philippians 1:27.
4. We are to **stand fast** *in the Lord*. Philippians 4:1 and 1st Thessalonians 3:8.
5. We are to **stand fast** *in the doctrine we have been taught*. 2nd Thessalonians 2:15.

Next, here are two areas in which we are to **"hold"** on with a firm grip.[21] *(Not every occurrence of these terms is listed. For further study, see the footnotes).*

1. We are to **hold** *the traditions (the substance of the teachings)*. 1 Corinthians 11:2, 2nd Thessalonians 2:15

---

[20] Meyers, Rick, (*Thayer's Greek Lexicon Dictionary*) E-Sword Software Version 11.1.0, Copyright ©2000-2017. G4739 stékō: *1) to stand firm*
[21] Meyers, Rick, (*Thayer's Greek Lexicon Dictionary*) E-Sword Software Version 11.1.0, Copyright ©2000-2017. G2722 katechō *1c) to hold fast, keep secure, keep firm possession of*

2. We are to **hold fast** *to our profession (or confession, oath to Christ)* of faith. Hebrews 10:23.

The "traditions we have been taught" are a reference to what Paul taught, not a reference to man-made traditions which are vain.[22] To grow in Christ, we must keep a firm grasp on the teaching of the mystery[23] that God revealed to Paul, and avoid any religious counterfeit of it. In fact, we are to withdraw from those who reject the truths that Paul labored to communicate. Not as an enemy but as a brother in Christ who we should love and encourage to live God's Word.[24]

Now, we will look at some important points concerning the word **"taught"** seen in 2 Thessalonians 2:15.[25]

1. Jesus Christ **taught** his disciples to diligently keep "…all things whatsoever I have commanded you." *(Matthew 28:2).*

---

[22] Colossians 2:6-9.
[23] Romans 16:25-26; Ephesians 3:1-9.
[24] 2 Thessalonians 3:6-15.
[25] Meyers, Rick, (*Thayer's Greek Lexicon Dictionary*) E-Sword Software Version 11.1.0, Copyright ©2000-2017. G1321 didaskó *1) to teach 1a) to hold discourse with others in order to instruct them, deliver didactic discourses*

2. Jesus Christ **taught** with authority. *(Mark 1:22).*
3. Jesus Christ combined teaching with healing. *(Matthew 4:23). (Paul also combined healing with his teachings whenever he could).*
4. God via the gift of holy spirit will **teach** you what you need to say is confrontational or ministering situations. *(Luke 12:12).*
5. Paul held nothing back that was profitable when he **taught** in Ephesus. *(Acts 20:20).* He made known to them everything he could, both in public and in the home fellowships.
6. Paul **taught** about the Kingdom of God and the things that concern Jesus Christ. *(Acts 28:31).* His teachings about the Kingdom of God likely included how the future reign of Christ, fits within God's Kingdom; which is over all including giving authority to His son and others.

Paul was methodical and diligent in his teaching style. The textual evidence shows that he developed a systematic, classroom style approach that took weeks to unfold. His classes covered enough to get the new believers "up and running" with living God's Word. He showed that Jesus fulfilled the law, and is the now resurrected Messiah, and he revealed the mystery which brought the Gentiles into the fold of the one spiritual body of Christ.

> **Acts 17:2-3, KJV**
> **2 And Paul, as his manner was, went in unto them, and three Sabbath days reasoned with them out of the scriptures,**
> **3 Opening and alleging, that Christ must needs have suffered, and risen again from the dead; and that this Jesus, whom I preach unto you, is Christ.**

Finally, we are to stand fast and hold firmly to what Paul *wrote* as well *(2 Thessalonians 2:15)*. None of us were present to hear Jesus or Paul in an oratory setting. What we have available to us is the *writings*, and people who help us by expounding upon them.

In the third usage of *"hellomai"* G138 we see that believers looked forward to the coming of the Christ, either the first coming or the second coming.

The third and final occurrence of *"hellomai"* G138 is in Hebrews 11:25. The context of Hebrews 11 reminds us that the Old Testament believers looked forward to the day of Christ. This hope helped them to stand upon the promises of God. They chose to demonstrate faith instead of caving into the pressures and pleasures of this world.

> **Hebrews 11: 24-26, KJV**
> **24 By faith Moses, when he was come to years, refused to be called the son of Pharaoh's daughter;**
> **25 Choosing** *(hellomai G138)* **rather to suffer affliction with the people of God, than to enjoy the pleasures of sin for a season;**
> **26 Esteeming the reproach of Christ greater riches than the treasures in Egypt: for he had respect unto the recompense of the reward.**

Again, all three occurrences of the root word *haireó* are in the middle voice *(hellomai)*, in which the subject acts upon itself, for itself, or to itself in some way.[26] Moses made the right choice because he understood the promise of God. He stood fast and held on to the truth. He did not waver in his mind.

In summery

We have been chosen and called to become members of the body of Christ and the family of God. Our

---

[26] In the Active voice, the subject does the action. In the Passive voice, the subject is acted upon by an object.

proper choice is to respond by acting upon ourselves – in the middle voice, so to speak – by renewing our minds. Both Jesus Christ and Paul exhorted the believers to hold fast to their teachings, and to go out and apply them in their lives. Doing so is how divine blessings unfold and are maximized. God has always wanted the very best for us – for His children – from the very beginning.

4: Our fellowship is with the Father and with the Son

1 John 1:1, 3 KJV
1 That which *(who)* was from the beginning, which *(who)* we have heard, which *(who)* we have seen with our eyes, which *(who)* we have looked upon, and our hands have handled, of the Word of life;
3 That which *(who)* we have seen and heard declare we unto you, that ye also may have fellowship with us: and truly our fellowship *is* with the Father, and with his Son Jesus Christ.

1 John 1:6-7 KJV
6 If we say that we have fellowship with him, and walk in darkness, we lie, and do not the truth:
7 But if we walk in the light, as he is in the light, *(walk as he is)* we have fellowship one with another, and the blood of Jesus Christ his Son cleanseth us from all sin.

1 John 2:6 KJV
6 He that saith he **abideth** in him ought himself also so to **walk,** even as he **walked.**

1 John 2:7 KJV
7 Brethren, I write no new commandment unto you, but an old commandment which ye had **from the beginning.** The old commandment is the word which ye have heard **from the beginning.**

When you read 1st John, there is an overwhelming theme that is brought to your attention. That theme is to walk in the light by abiding in the light, or to **"walk as he is."** In 1st John 1:7 there is a repetition of the phrase **"in the light"** and the word or words in front of each repeated phrase are: **"walk,"** and **"as he is."** Isn't that interesting? We are to walk "in the light" as he is "in the light." We are to **"walk as he is"** walking **"in the light!"**

Another interesting repetition is the word **"which"** or **"that which,"** that should be translated **"who"** since is describing some qualities of Jesus Christ, who is also the major topic or context in this section. 1st John 1:2 confirms this as being the major topic being a parenthesis between verse 1 and 3, and verses 6-10 further confirm this by referring to Jesus Christ in almost every phrase as our mediator so we can continue to have fellowship with God and Jesus Christ. And we do this by **walking in the light, as he walked in the light.** The light being the precepts and tenets from God's Word. Here is the list of things mentioned in verses 1.

1. Who was **from the beginning**. *(in God's foreknowledge (Gen. 3:15)*
2. Who **we have heard**. *(The teachings of Jesus Christ)*
3. Who **we have seen**. *(eye witnesses)*
4. Who **we have looked upon**. *(eye witnesses)*
5. Who **our hands has handled**. *(they have touched him as another human would touch others during daily activities)*

1st John 1:2 describes **who** verse 1 is taking about in terms of God's foreknowledge to send a saviour, and that they are not only eye witnesses, but witnesses by their operation of the gift holy spirit also, by the phrase "**…and we have seen *it*, and bear witness,**"

> **1 John 1:2 KJV**
> **2 (For the life was manifested,** *(Jesus Christ)* **and we have seen *it*, and bear witness,** *(by eye witness and speaking in tongues)*[27] **and shew unto you that eternal**

---

[27] Arbib, Peter., *(20+ Benefits Speaking in Tongues Has for You)*, Sound Wisdom Publications, Camby, IN. 2018 p. 57-64, Chapter 4: Speaking in tongues is God bearing witness with our spirit that are His children.

life, which was with the Father, and was manifested unto us;)

That is: what we have been taught via God's Word to **walk in the light** by the teachings of Jesus Christ and the teachings of Paul concerning living the great mystery, not just in our personal walk but living the great mystery as a collective body of believers, the one body. Where everyone is contributing their long suits with the believers in their area and supplying their part in the one body as a group as each one is living in the light of God's Word and giving that to their fellow believers.

There are some key words we want to look at. The first one is the word **"abide"** which is used 23 times in 18 verses in 1st John. The only other book that has more uses is the Gospel of John where is used 41 times in 34 verses. A huge repetition like this is a key word we need to look at. Because it is repeated so many times in these two books, this repetition is telling us that one of the *main themes* of these books is about **"abiding in His Word,"** and our understanding of these books will revolve around this theme. This is one way God protects His Word from private interpretation. These two books in the Bible will give us the main instructions on "how" to abide in God's Word as sons of God with a vital relationship with God and with His son Jesus Christ. These books will also show us the great keys in how to renew our mind. It will show us great keys in how to make the **right** choice. The Gospel of John shows us Jesus Christ as **the son of God** and how he acted as such. 1st John shows us as sons of God how to keep our vital relationship active and well and in good standing.

Other related words in the context we will look are the words **"walk,"** and **"fellowship."** Another theme in 1st John that revolves around the main theme to **"abide in Him"** is that Jesus Christ has cleansed *(purified)* us from all present/future sin *(disobedience)* and He has forgiven us from all *present/future* sin by walking in Him. He will not only purify us of our present sin *(disobedience)* by way of **"walking in Him,"** He will also forgive us of that sin *(disobedience)* by **"walking in Him."** This is a benefit of **"abiding in Him,"** when we do get off course, and then get back on track, our mistake is cleansed from us, and we are forgiven of that mistake.

Within this theme of "forgiveness" in the New Testament, we are encouraged to forgive others for their current mistakes as Christ has forgiven us for our current mistakes in our Christian walk. This is also a part of living *in* the fellowship of the one body that we all members of regardless of what Christian church we are a part of, and what level of understanding anyone has! Which all revolves around the main theme of **"abiding in Him."**

So, you can see this chapter will get into a large topic that is vitally important we all understand and grasp the big picture past your individual Christian walk. By growing into your calling in Christ in the *one body*; as a member who is now *giving* to the *one body*, the fellowship can now benefit from your long-suit, as others who are also *giving* their contribution to the *one body* as a collective of likeminded believers building *the unity of spirit* in the *one body*.

This is the goal we should have according to Romans 12ff *(the great chapter on living the renewed mind as part of the one body)*. 1st John lays out how important our fellowship is with each other and with God and Jesus Christ and lays out major keys to maintain and live in that fellowship as an individual believer and as a contributing member of the *one body* which is something God has wanted from the beginning.

And the phrase **"from the beginning"** shows up more times in 1st John than any other book in the Bible. It is used 9 times in 7 verses so, we will look at the topic this phrase is surrounded with, bearing in mind what the main theme is for 1st John is "abiding in Jesus Christ."

Let's get started, though I will not teach in the order in which the words or phrases appear as you read 1st John. Instead I will work them so that I can teach on the major concepts first, and then add the supporting words or phrases which should make easier to grasp the larger picture that is underlying our Christian walk in Christ.

There are many uses of the word **"walk"** in the New Testament, but we'll look at some of the uses that help define this word beyond the dictionary definition, and look at the some of the categories this word is used in.

The word "walk" in the Greek is the word "peripateo" (G4043) and is pronounced "per-ee-pat-eh'-o" and is the verb form and means: *(I) To tread or walk about, generally to walk. In Rom 6:4 it is used figuratively as describing a manner of life.: (II) Figuratively: to live or pass one's life,* (1722 "en") *in the dative, of state or condition also of rule or manner:* (Rom. 6:4, *walking* "in newness of life," 2nd Cor. 4:2, *walking* "in craftiness," Eph. 2:2, *walked* "according to the course of this world.)"[28]

Thayer's Greek New Testament Dictionary-E-Sword Version and paperback version: *1) to walk 1a) to make one's way, progress; to make do use of opportunities 1b) Hebrew for, to live 1b1) to regulate one's life 1b2) to conduct one's self. ...* (from the paperback

---

[28] Zodhiates, Spiros, Th.D., *(The Complete Word Study Dictionary: New Testament),* AMG Publishers, Chattanooga, TN., Revised 1993. p. 1148, ref: 4043, I, II.

version): ... *(to live a life conformed the union entered into with Christ, see Colossians 2:6)*[29]

Romans 6:4 KJV
4 Therefore we are buried with him by baptism into death: that like as Christ was raised up from the dead by the glory of the Father, even so we also should walk in newness of life.

Because Christ was raised from the dead and lives with a new spiritual body and a new way of life, we also should live in a new manner of lifestyle that reflects our new state of eternal life that God has given us with our gift of holy spirit. This is part of the renewed mind; we were buried with Christ and we were raised with Christ when we got born-again. That is: He took our place for us when He died, so legally we died with Him. When we received the gift of holy of spirit, we were given the token of eternal life, which also guarantees we will receive a new spiritual body like His. Therefore, we were raised up together with Him legally.

---

[29] Meyers, Rick, *(Thayer's Greek Lexicon Dictionary)* E-Sword Software Version 11.1.0, Copyright ©2000-2017. Ref: 4043
Thayer, Joseph H., *(Thayer's Greek-English Lexicon of the New Testament)*, Baker Books House, Grand Michigan, 24th printing. p. 504, ref: 4043 2nd column, lines 21-22.

Therefore, we should endeavour to walk in the newness of what we were given through Jesus Christ. Which involves two parts:

1. Changing our habits and lifestyle to live like Jesus Christ,
2. And to operate God's power in our life like Jesus Christ did. Our gift holy spirit gives us the ability to tap into and to use God's power for healing and receiving revelation just like Jesus Christ did.

By renewing our mind *(thoughts)* and changing our habits to live God's Word, *and by* operating our gift of holy spirit, we will also live like Jesus Christ did.

The phrase **"... even so we also should walk in newness of life"** is worth looking at for a moment so we can determine "who" is supposed to take away our old habits we have and replace them with new habits, so we can "walk in newness in life." Well, what does it say? **"we** *(you)* **also should walk..."** Who does the walking which involves changing your habits in the end? "We" *(or you)* should walk, **"YOU" should walk.** You are the one who must get rid of your bad habits and replace them with new habits that line up with God's Word. God will not take away your bad habits for you, but God will show you what to replace the bad habit within His

Word. It is up to you to change by your freedom of will.

This is a huge key to have "fellowship with the Father and with the Son." The main topic we are looking at in this chapter is God wanted fellowship from the beginning with mankind. Man lost it, God had a plan to restore it, Jesus Christ fulfilled God's plan to restore mankind's fellowship with God.

In the next two uses we will look at a figure of speech of repetition that forms a "bookend"[30] or a topical paragraph that will further explain the phrase that is repeated at the beginning and the end of the paragraph. This kind of repetition, a "bookend," will separate out a topic for added emphasis in the larger section it is used in.

> **Romans 8:1-4 KJV**
> **1** *There* *is* **therefore now no condemnation to them which are in Christ Jesus, who walk not after the flesh, but after the Spirit.**
> **2** For the law of the Spirit of life in Christ Jesus hath made me free from the law of sin and death.

---

[30] Nessle, Jon O., *(Repetitions-Revealing a Hidden Key to the Heart of Scripture)*, Next Reformation Publishing Co. Plainfield, https://www.academia.edu/24932331/Repetitions_A_Key_to_Understanding_the_Heart_of_Scripture

3 For what the law could not do, in that it was weak through the flesh, God sending his own Son in the likeness of sinful flesh, and for sin, condemned sin in the flesh:
4 That the righteousness of the law might be fulfilled in us, **who walk not after the flesh, but after the Spirit.**

Nobody could walk in the righteousness of the Law because we were weak in the flesh and carnally minded. We thought and acted on worldly things, not godly things from the spirit. But Jesus Christ who lived in the flesh, condemned sin, After Jesus Christ was baptized by John at age 30, *(the start of His ministry officially)*, the spirit that God gave Him led Him to the wilderness to be tempted by every temptation Satan had to throw at Him hoping Jesus Christ would be tricked and fall prey to at least one temptation. If He did, then Jesus Christ would have failed to redeem mankind right then and there. But Jesus Christ did not fall prey to any of the temptations and defeated Satan's power that day.

But it was still up to Jesus Christ to continue to walk by the spirit by keeping His thoughts and actions on God's Word. He still had to keep His renewed mind stance and make moment by moment choices to do God's Word and not to be tricked by the circumstances to walk by the flesh that would result in making the wrong choices.

When we receive the gift of holy spirit, we now can walk in *the righteousness of the law* and fulfil the law as we choose to walk in the spirit, by renewing our mind *(thoughts and actions)* to God's Word and by operating our gift of holy spirit at will. When we walk by the spirit, we are made free from the letter of the Law because we are walking by a higher calling, the calling to love God and to love others with God's love, which has always been not only our calling, but the calling of all believers from the beginning. If we walk in God's love towards others, we will fulfil the Law, Jesus Christ made that available to everyone that has been given God's gift to mankind, holy spirit. This is what this repetition of this phrase emphasises, when we walk by the spirit, when we are spiritually minded, when we renew our thoughts and actions to live by God's Word.

> **1 Corinthians 7:17 KJV**
> **17 But as God hath distributed to every man, as the Lord hath called every one, so let him walk. And so ordain I in all churches.**
>
> **Ephesians 2:10 KJV**

10 For we are his workmanship, created in Christ Jesus unto good works, which God hath before ordained that we should walk in them.

Every believer has a calling, a ministry, a long suit that will bless the one body. To figure out what your calling is, you will have to start serving the believers in areas that you are inspired to help in. As you grow in service you will start to see what your longsuits are and find your calling, your ministry, which blesses the one body of Christ. If you don't endeavour to continue to grow and serve in the church, then your calling won't come into fruition, you will have a ministry, but to no effect. There are not only ruling ministries, but there are also service or support ministries. All of them are important.

So far, we have these categories that we are to walk in.

1. Romans 6:4, **"walk in newness of life"**
2. Romans 8:1, 4, **"walk after the spirit"**
3. 1st Corinthians 7:17, Ephesians 2:10, **"walk" according to your calling** *(ministry)* **from God**

Galatians 5:16-17 KJV
16 *This* **I say then, Walk in the Spirit, and ye shall not fulfil the lust of the flesh.**

17 For the flesh lusteth against the Spirit, and the Spirit against the flesh: and these are contrary the one to the other: so that ye cannot do the things that ye would.

There are two ways to walk, by the spirit, and by the flesh. You can't walk by both at the same time. You can only walk one-way at a time, either by the spirit, or by the flesh. It is a choice you make every day, just like Jesus Christ had to make every day. When the Pharisees tempted Him with trick questions, He had to answer them with a question that was impossible to answer without the answer causing them to look guilty in some way. This is one-way Jesus Christ walked by the spirit, so he did not sin, or answer their question in an ungodly, or revengeful vile way.

Here is the record that shows Jesus Christ walking by the spirit by His choice to do the right thing, the godly thing, to love her and forgive her, and not do the ungodly thing to condemn and kill her because The Law says to. Jesus Christ walked with God's love towards her. This was a choice Jesus Christ made instead of carrying out *the letter of the Law*, Jesus Christ carried out *the spirit of the Law* and loved and forgave her.

John 8:3-11 KJV

3 And the scribes and Pharisees brought unto him a woman taken in adultery; and when they had set her in the midst,

4 They say unto him, Master, this woman was taken in adultery, in the very act.

5 Now Moses in the law commanded us, that such should be stoned: but what sayest thou?

6 This they said, tempting him, that they might have to accuse him. But Jesus stooped down, and with *his* finger wrote on the ground, *as though he heard them not.*

7 So when they continued asking him, he lifted up himself, and said unto them, He that is without sin among you, let him first cast a stone at her.

8 And again he stooped down, and wrote on the ground.

9 And they which heard *it*, being convicted by *their own* conscience, went out one by one, beginning at the eldest, *even* unto the last: and Jesus was left alone, and the woman standing in the midst.

10 When Jesus had lifted up himself, and saw none but the woman, he said unto her, Woman, where are those thine

**accusers? hath no man condemned thee?
11 She said, No man, Lord. And Jesus said unto her, Neither do I condemn thee: go, and sin no more.**

Before we were born-again, and before we had the gift of holy spirit, we belonged to Satan. The worlds power and dominion were given to him from Adam's disobedience. Satan had control over the things of the world and could influence our lives through these areas, and we had no control over it. We were Satan's because we had no power to stop him. We were in darkness, without a clue about what was really going on when bad things happened to us.

But when we became born-again, we received the gift of holy spirit, and became the children of light, and we were given the ability to stop the attacks of Satan and have dominion and power once again over the world. But, only to the extent we walk in the light of God's Word by renewing our mind *(our thoughts and actions)* will we have this power and dominion over Satan and the world. Here are some great verses comparing darkness to light in various ways.

Just a reminder, this chapter is on fellowship with God and with Jesus Christ, walking in the light will keep us in fellowship; walking in darkness

will cause us to break the connection we have when we are in fellowship.

Fellowship is a choice we make every moment of each day by our thoughts and actions, if they are ungodly, then we walk in darkness and are out of fellowship. If our thoughts and actions are godly, then we walk in the light and we have fellowship with each other and with God and Jesus Christ.

> Ephesians 5:8 KJV
> 8 For ye were sometimes darkness, but now *are ye* light in the Lord: walk as children of light:
>
> John 8:12 KJV
> 12 Then spake Jesus again unto them, saying, I am the light of the world: he that followeth me shall not walk in darkness, but shall have the light of life.
>
> John 12:46 KJV
> 46 I am come a light into the world, that whosoever believeth on me should not abide in darkness.
>
> Acts 26:18 KJV
> 18 To open their eyes, *and* to turn *them* from darkness to light, and *from* the power of Satan unto God, that they may receive forgiveness of sins, and

inheritance among them which are sanctified by faith that is in me.

2 Corinthians 4:6 KJV
6 For God, who commanded the light to shine out of darkness, hath shined in our hearts, to *give* the light of the knowledge of the glory of God in the face of Jesus Christ.

1 Thessalonians 5:5 KJV
5 Ye are all the children of light, and the children of the day: we are not of the night, nor of darkness.

1 John 1:5 KJV
5 This then is the message which we have heard of him, and declare unto you, that God is light, and in him is no darkness at all.

4A: REPETITIONS, VERSE STRUCTURE, & PHRASE PAIRS

1st John contains the largest concentration of the Greek word translated **"walk"** in the New Testament. Therefore, this book will set the foundation for what it is to **"walk"** and to have fellowship, and what broken fellowship looks like. We will be studying 1st John 1:6-10 in a very detailed way to point out "repetitions," "verse structure, and "phrase pairs" to show us vital keys on "how" to **"walk in the light"** as Jesus Christ **"walked in the light."** I recommend you slow down and grasp each break down that is presented in this sub-chapter.

> 1 John 1:6-7 KJV
> 6 **If we** say that we have fellowship with him, and **walk** in darkness, we lie, and do not the truth:
> 7 But **if we walk** in the light, as he is in the light, we have fellowship one with another, and the blood of Jesus Christ his Son cleanseth us from all sin.

These two verses give a comparison of walking in darkness and walking in the light in relationship to having fellowship or not having fellowship with God. There is a conditional clause that tells us it is our choice which way we decide to walk in darkness or in the light, and the outcome of each choice. The conditional clause is: **"if we"** in both verses above. 1st John 1:6 is the waking in darkness, for example.

> 1st John 1:6 KJV
> 6 If we <u>say</u>... we have fellowship... and walk in darkness, we lie and do not the truth.

It is self-evident then that we are out of fellowship despite what we profess in our lie. This will be one of the repetitions we will look at in a moment along with the conclusions of the actions we should take. Typically, there would be a **"then"** clauses to supply the conclusion, but in this section of scripture in 1st John 1:6-10 the **"verse structure"** of these verses will supply the **"then"** clauses instead.

Here is another verse in 1st John 2:4a that says the same basic truth from 1st John 1:6a, but states it differently in essence:

Stating you are in:

- **"fellowship"** or stating that you **"know Him by experience"** when in fact you are
- **"walking in darkness,"** or **"not keeping His commandments"**

Gives us more evidence that 1st John is about **"walking in Him"** or **"not walking in Him"** as a major theme.

> **1 John 2:4 KJV**
> **4 He that saith, I know him, and keepeth not his commandments, is a liar, and the truth is not in him.**

You can't **"walk"** in darkness and **"walk"** in the light at the same time, you must make a choice, if you choose to walk in the light as He is in the light, then you will have fellowship with not only God and Jesus Christ, but you will also have fellowship with each other; the other believers in the one body of Christ as 1st John 1:7 declares.

> **1 John 2:5-6 KJV**
> **5 But whoso keepeth his word, in him verily is the love of God perfected: hereby know we that we are in him.**
> **6 He that saith he abideth in him ought himself also so to walk, even as he walked.**

If we walk as He walked, as we profess, then God's love is perfected in us, and we know by experience we are in Him. We are in fellowship. My suggestion is you read each sub-section below a few times each before you read the next sub-section so that you really get it!

4a:1 Verse Structure in Out Line Form

Before I go to the last few verses the word **"walk"** is used in, I want to share why I believe 1st John 1:6-10 is one of the greatest sections on what causes our relationship to strive or stumble with God and His son Jesus Christ and the believers. And what we need to do so we can repair our relationship *(fellowship)* with God and His son Jesus Christ and the believers when needed. The best way to do this is to show you some of the grammatical structure in a simplified manner. I will list the outline structure, the repetitions, and the similar phases so you can see what God has emphasized in an easier to understand form.

Verse 1st John 1:6-10 is a small section that is defined by several grammatical structural keys.

1: **Outline Structure:** *means how similar or opposites verses connect when you compare the matching outline structure. That is: A's can be connected, B's can be connected, etc. You can read A's together to see the comparison. Here are how the pairs work together.*

A, B, C, B, A
(A) verses 6 and 10,
(B) verses 7 and 9,
(C) verse 8

"A"
1 John 1:6 *If we say that we have fellowship with him, and walk in darkness, we lie, and do not the truth:*
1 John 1:10 *If we say that we have not sinned, we make him a liar, and his word is not in us.*

The essence is that if we say we have fellowship or say we have not sinned, we make us and Him a liar, and the truth of His word is not in us. (the next pair of "B's" show us how to resolve the pair of "A's" above)

"B"

1 John 1:7 *But if we walk in the light, as he is in the light, we have fellowship one with another, and the blood of Jesus Christ his Son cleanseth us from all sin.*
1 John 1:9 *If we confess our sins, he is faithful and just to forgive us our sins, and to cleanse us from all unrighteousness.*

The essence is if we walk in the light after walking in darkness, we will get back in fellowship. A part of walking in the light is to admit we have made a mistake to God, and Jesus Christ will forgive us and cleanse us from our unrighteousness, this will reestablish our fellowship with God and Jesus Christ, and with one another.

"C"

1 John 1:8 *If we say that we have no sin, we deceive ourselves, and the truth is not in us.*

*Then we only have one verse for "C," and this verse verifies that even though we are saved and have eternal life and we can't lose that, we are still going to sin or break fellowship, so don't cop an attitude of being "holier than thou," deceiving yourself. We all need to reestablish our broken fellowship throughout our Christian walk through Jesus Christ's forgiveness and cleansing of our unrighteous actions. This section IS NOT ABOUT SALVATION! It is about MAINTAINING FELLOWSHIP (OUR ON-GOING RELATIONSHIP) **AFTER** SALVATION!*[31] *If you read the verse before and after 1st John 1:8, verse 8*

---

[31] 1 John 1:3
3 That which we have seen and heard declare we unto you, **that ye also may have** fellowship **with us: and truly our** fellowship *is* **with the Father, and with his Son Jesus Christ.**

covers both sides… being out of fellowship and getting back in fellowship in two different explanations.

4a:2 Repetitions

2: **Repetitions** *define the subject or the topic in a section; what God wants to bring to our attention or emphasize. In this section, what we say about our fellowship and sin is to be honest (no holier than thou attitude), and realize that after we are saved, we still need forgiveness because we will never act perfectly in the flesh, and we shall (absolutely) break our fellowship when we act in an unrighteous way, and then we need Jesus Christ to forgive us and cleanse us from that current sin (unrighteousness).*

"If we" is used a total of 5 times, "if we say we" 3x). The largest repetition is the phrase "if we" used 5 times. This phrase puts our fellowship, or relationship squarely in OUR COURT. "If we" puts our fellowship and relationship in *our daily choices from living God's Word or rejecting God's Word in every decision we make that results in action, (right actions or wrong actions), this* puts our fellowship, our relationship in *the category of our RENEWED MIND that determines whether or not we will live or reject God's Word. That means that we are 100% responsible for our* state *of fellowship, our* state *of the relationship (not sonship) we have with God and Jesus Christ.*

This section in 1st John 1:6-10 main topic is about our *attitude and actions thinking now that we are saved, we cannot sin. This section reminds us that we can still sin even after salvation, and that we still need forgiveness and cleansing from Jesus Christ to maintain* our *fellowship, our relationship (not our salvation). The repetitions bear this* out. The repetitions guide us to what the main topic is in this section.

"Lie/Liar"

V6/V10 *If we say we are in fellowship or have no sin, we are a liar. We are not always in fellowship, there are times we make the wrong decision and that is walking in darkness or walking in unrighteousness. That will break off our fellowship.*

"We have fellowship"

V6/V7 *If we walk in the light, that is: confess our sin (wrong decision, broken fellowship) we will be forgiven and cleansed by Jesus Christ as our mediator to God, so we can have fellowship once again with one another and with God and Jesus Christ. It is interesting to note that being out of fellowship with God also effects our fellowship or relationships with the believers! By acknowledging our sin, Jesus Christ restores not only our fellowship or relationship with God, but also with our fellow believers.*

"If we say we"

V6/V8/V10 *If we say we have fellowship, no sin, and have not sinned (attitude being "holier than thou"), we walk in darkness, we deceive ourselves, and make Him a liar. We don't do the truth, the truth is not in us, the Word is not in us.*

"If we"

V6/V7/V8/V9/V10 *This repetition reminds us that we are the ones responsible to walk in the truth, to live God's Word, to make the right decisions based on God's Word. This repetition gives us what not to do and what to do to sustain our fellowship with God, Jesus Christ, and the fellow believers. It is our choice, 100%, every day, every hour, every minute, every second. This is how the renewed* *mind works, when we read in God's Word what we need to do in place of what we used to do, and we change our mind to do what God's Word says, the corrected action is the renewed mind and we are in fellowship again.*

"Cleanseth us/Cleanse us"

__V7/V9__ Both verses have the same Greek word "katharizo" (G2511), but verse 9 adds "forgiveness" to the equation. Forgiveness is used for the "absolution" of the sin, and "Cleansing" is used for the purging from the unrighteousness in our heart. So, our sin and the unrighteousness in our heart from the sin is purged in God's eyes. This should alleviate (or release us) from any quilt (when we renew our mind to believe what Jesus Christ does for us right now for our present sins), allowing us to be restored in our fellowship with God, Jesus Christ, and the believers.

As we find areas we need to change in our life, and we find the solutions as we study God's Word and change our actions to match what God's Word says. We will be purging our old, bad, unrighteous habits to live the new righteous habits that will keep our fellowship with God. Forgiveness is a very big deal with God, and we should also give out forgiveness to fellow believers and others when needed, so that person can forgive themselves and be released from any quilt that their sin is causing. That is being cleansed, it involves <u>forgiveness</u> to get the cleansing started, so it can be purged from a person's mind in the sense of not feeling bad or guilty of their wrongdoing. When a person can get to that point in their thinking (believing), they can start to live without that <u>sin-consciousness</u> anymore and move on with the right attitude and behaviors.

4a:3 Similar phrases

*3: **Similar phrases** Although these are similar phrases, we will need to look at the preceding phrase to help us with understanding what it means. Many times, if we just slow down and ask ourselves; is there more here than just "principles?" I am referring to the psychology or attitude that can be extracted from the verse. This is what we are going to look at in these three similar phrases. I will include the preceding phrase to give us a better starting point. As you will see, each phrase is a progression in understanding.*

V6/V8/V10 "phrases with the understanding of lying"

"*we lie*, and do not the truth:"

V6: This is the simplest explanation where most of us stop in understanding. We tell a lie, why? To hide the truth from others, to make them think "we have it together." We know we don't have it together, but we won't admit it. Because of "pride," and "ego," and possibly promoting our perceived "reputation." Therefore, we <u>did not do the truth (or say the truth)</u>. "If we <u>say</u> we (always) have fellowship with him, and (but) we walk in darkness. We lie, and do not (say) the truth."

"*we deceive ourselves*, and the truth is not in us:"

*V8: Verse 8 takes the concept to a deeper level. Verse 6 said: "If we <u>say</u> we (always) have **fellowship** with him, and (but) we walk in darkness. We lie, and do not (say) the truth."*

*Verse 8 now takes the fellowship and replaces it with **"have no sin."** If we (say we) have no sin, Verse 6: Then we (say we) are (always) in fellowship with him. See it?*

*And then verse 8 takes verse 6's "we lie" and replaces it with **"we deceive ourselves."** The next level of lying in understanding. When we lie, we know it, therefore we are also deceiving ourselves by telling a lie, then verse 8 takes the phrase in verse 6 **"we do not the truth,"** and replaces it with **"the truth is not in us."** Going a step further in understanding and telling us we are <u>not holding</u> the truth <u>in our mind</u>. That is why we did not do <u>or live</u> the truth in verse 6. Verse 8 shows us the reality of falsely claiming we are always in fellowship, is falsely claiming we have no sin anymore because of what Jesus Christ did for us. Remember, this is about FELLOWSHIP, not SALVATION! Fellowship is your RELATIONSHIP after SALVATION, so stop confusing them and thinking there are the same. FELLOWSHIP and SALVATION are not the same!*

That belief is walking in darkness, and not realizing that if we have a physical body, we will always have sin nature in us, and we must decide every day either to "do the truth" or to "not do the truth." Paul had the same issue with himself![32] *Yes, Jesus Christ did die for our sin nature because we are descendants from Adam. Yes, Jesus Christ did cleanse us from all rightness, not in our physical body, but spiritually, in God's eyes, because He gave us a perfect spirit as a gift to overcome our sin nature (SALVATION). God sees our perfect spirit within us as the real us. But we still need forgiveness and cleansing for current sins, (for continued FELLOWSHIP) look at V7/V9 above again. We will not be sin free in our physical body until we shed it, and receive our new spiritual body, along with our new mind, and new knowledge at the return of Christ. In the mean-time we need to change our habits that are contrary to God's Word and replace them with habits that agree with*

---

[32] Roman 7ff,

God's Word, so we can live in our spiritual righteousness in our physical being, thus being in harmony and in fellowship. This is living in godliness.[33] Living the doctrine of the mystery of godliness – CHRIST IN YOU - is carried out with our thoughts first, then with our accompanying actions in our physical being. The renewed mind.

"we make him a liar, and his word is not in us:"

V10: *This verse gives us the bottom line on what is happening spiritually. It is the last level of the truth about our lie. When God's Word is not <u>IN</u> us, (although we know the truth and don't do the truth – V6), we make Jesus Christ a liar with our lie. We are purposely hiding the truth in our lie. That is why His Word is not <u>IN</u> us, that is, it is not living in our soul, it is not real to us in our life, we have not truly changed our thoughts to act on His Word. We know it, and we know it is true, but we have decided not to live it quite yet. We may not be ready, or we purposely don't want to live it, so we lie. The truth is not <u>IN</u> us yet.*

V8/V10 "Phrases with the idea of not having/doing sin"

"If we say that we no sin:"

V8: *If we say we have no sin in the sense we literally have no sin in our life, we are leading ourselves away from the truth of God's Word. ("… we deceive ourselves…"). You*

---

[33] 1 Timothy 3:16
16 And without controversy great is **the mystery of godliness:** ~~God~~ who was manifest in the flesh, justified in the Spirit, seen of angels, preached unto the Gentiles, believed on in the world, received up into glory.
1 Timothy 6:3
3 If any man teach otherwise, and consent not to wholesome words, *even* the words of our Lord Jesus Christ, and to **the doctrine which is according to godliness;**

must know the truth to walk away from the truth, thus deceiving yourself.

What can cause this kind of thinking? Not acknowledging what Paul acknowledged concerning the battle we all have between our spiritually renewed mind and our carnal unrenewed mind. The constant battle to <u>do the right thing</u>, and not allow our carnal mind to <u>do the wrong thing</u>. But even Paul says there are times he did the wrong thing, though against his will (against his spiritually renewed mind) to do the right thing. Paul realized that until the return, he would at times do the wrong thing, but he also understood when he renewed his mind to do the Word, that is where he could serve God. Trying to serve God in the flesh (with our carnal mind -thoughts, - our sin nature) is not available, he knew his flesh (earthly ways of doing things) resulted in acting by his sin nature. He knew that Jesus Christ did not take away any of his carnal thoughts, his sin nature.

Getting rid of our carnal thoughts, our sin nature 100% will only happen when Christ returns, and we receive our new spiritual body and mind. In the interim, we need to serve God with our renewed mind. If we had no sin, carnal thoughts, our sin nature from our mind, then we would have no need to <u>renew</u> our mind, we would have a perfectly renewed mind NOW! This is NOT available until the return of Christ.[34] *You may want to look up the Greek*

---

[34] Romans 7:23-25 But I see another law in my members, warring against the law of my mind, and bringing me into captivity to the law of sin which is in my members. 24 O wretched man that I am! who shall deliver me from the body of this death? 25 I thank God through Jesus Christ our Lord. So then with the mind I myself serve the law of God; but with the flesh the law of sin.

words G5426: phroneō, (understand/are wise in). G5427: phronēma, the thoughts or purposes-in a specific sense.

"If we say that we have not sinned:"

V10: *This phrase is slightly different from the aforementioned phrase. The first phrase from verse 8 says "... we <u>have no</u> sin...," the phrase in Verse 10 says "... we <u>have not</u> sinned...." One is saying "I have no sin in me." The other is saying "I have not sinned at all." Covering both the attitude and deed of no sin is in me. This is impossible since Christ has not returned yet to replace our flesh and blood body with our new spiritual body. As the rest of the verse 6 and 10 point out, we are deceiving ourselves and making Jesus Christ a liar because we are confusing our spiritual wholeness that He gave us and applying it to our carnal sin nature, which will never be spiritually whole. Jesus Christ did not take away our carnal sin nature, but His work did make our sin nature void IN GOD'S EYES. We still have it, and what we choose to act on will determine whether we act on God's Word, or we act on our sin nature.* ==God has always given mankind a choice to live His Word or reject His Word from the beginning.== *We decide by renewing our mind (thoughts) or by giving in to our carnal sin nature. If we lie by telling others or ourselves that we can no longer sin because we have no sin in us anymore by Jesus Christ, we don't understand the truth of God's Word concerning our spiritual forgiveness and cleansing, or Salvation vs Fellowship.*

This leads to believing God can take away our sin nature, like lying, or stealing, or cheating, or smoking, or cussing.

Romans 8:5 For they that are after the flesh do mind *(understand/are wise in)* the things of the flesh; but they that are after the Spirit *(understand/are wise in)* the things of the Spirit.

All these sin nature activities are under "the renewed mind" category, that is, we are the ones who must take away these sin nature activities by changing our mind to stop doing them, not God.

How to turn our lie and deception around and regain fellowship is a twostep process in V7 and V9 in the "B" parts of the outline structure of these 5 verses.

"But if we walk in the light...we have fellowship:"

V7: *If we walk (or conduct ourselves) as Jesus Christ conducts Himself, we will be back in fellowship (the main context of 1st John). Look at the words "if we walk," the phrase **"if we"** starts a conditional clause that places this change ON US to start the process of changing our carnal habits to habits that reflect the truth of God's Word. God does not and will not take away lying, for instance, **we are the ones who must not lie** when we have the urge or the opportunity to lie. **We must** consciously stop ourselves from telling a lie, and consciously tell the truth instead. That is what "renewing your mind" is.*

"If we confess our sins...he is faithful to forgive us:"

V9: *the second step is to admit our mistake and error in judgement. What good is it to change your actions without taking responsibility for your actions that were in error? That is no more than trying to "please men,"[35] that is, look good in your actions without admitting you were wrong inwardly. God looks on the heart, and knows your heart, if you want true forgiveness from man and God, you must take responsibility and admit your mistakes, and then your*

---

[35] Ephesians 6:6
6 Not with eyeservice, as menpleasers; but as the servants of Christ, doing the will of God from the heart;

renewed mind responses will be genuine in man's eyes and in God's eyes. God will always forgive you, so you can move on without the thoughts from guilt or disappointing God. This is necessary for you to get back on the road to fellowship. The next two pairs are what God will do in response to confessing our sin (broken fellowship in the context).

We are to admit we were wrong in what we did and start to change our actions to get back to doing what is right in accordance with God's Word. This includes a genuine change of heart to be honest or truthful.

God purifies us in His sight from all wrong actions and moral wrongs we have committed when we admit and start to change our mind to do the right thing (renewed mind in action) as V7 and V9 phrases below point out. V7: our wrong action, V9: our wrong moral attitude.

"cleanseth us from all sin:"

V7: Jesus Christ paid the price for our redemption from Adam's disobedience and for our current sin nature. So, we could be forgiven as the aforementioned phrases have shown us. Part of our forgiveness includes God through the finished work of His son Jesus Christ cleansing us all our current and future works stemming from our sin nature. When God forgives us, He also forgets our wrong actions forever, never to be brought up again.[36] *Therefore, we can*

---

[36] Jeremiah 31:34 (This is "to" Israel and Judah, not the Church, but we can apply the principle of "forgiveness and forgetting")
34 And they shall teach no more every man his neighbour, and every man his brother, saying, Know the LORD: for they shall all know me, from the least of them unto the greatest of them, saith the LORD: **for I will forgive their iniquity, and I will remember their sin no more.**

also keep our mind clean from the wrong things we have done and admitted and changed our ways to do the right thing by thinking what God through Jesus Christ has done for us and believing it!

"cleanse us from all unrighteousness:"

V9: This similar phrase can also include our moral attitude, our motivation that guides our actions. God can cleanse our heart from these as we renew our thoughts to act on God's Word. We can't [act] on truth and error at the same time. We can only act on one or the other, this is our choice from the beginning that God has given us. When we walk by the spirit of God in us, we cannot walk by the flesh's sin nature at the same time. This is how we are made free from the law of the flesh, or sin nature, with each sin we stop doing by doing what God's Word says instead. So, we are cleansed in God's eyes by what Jesus Christ did for us and will also be cleansed from the current and future sins by keeping our thoughts on living God's Word and therefore we will not walk in the flesh in those areas. We will never be 100% free from walking in the flesh physically though. That will only happen when we are gathered together and we receive our new spiritual body, along with our new knowledge, and powers.

**Romans 8:1-2: 1 There is therefore now no condemnation to them which are in Christ Jesus, who walk not after the flesh, but after the Spirit.
2 For the law of the Spirit of life in Christ Jesus hath made me free from the law of sin and death.**

The parallels in the above pairs of the verses as seen by their outline structure

4a:4 Like Phrases or Connected Phrases

Like Phrases: Repetitions: "if we say," Set "a"

A) **V6a) If we say** we (always) have fellowship with him and walk in darkness
B) V7a) But if we walk in the light
C) **V8a) If we say** we have no sin
B) V9a) If we confess our sins
A) **V10a) If we say** we have not sinned

The logic of the above A,C,A breakdown

"C" is the general truth
"A" are the specific levels of "C"
("B's" are how to get back in the truth)

V8a) **we say we have no sin.** (how? V6A, V10A)
 V6a) we say we are always in fellowship with God and walk in darkness
 V10a) we say we have not sinned anymore

How do we get back in fellowship with Him?

V7a) we walk in the light
V9a) we confess (admit) our sin

1st Set of Similar Phrases: Set "b"

A) V6b) we lie
B) V7b) we have fellowship one with another
C) V8b) we deceive ourselves

B) V9b) he is faithful and just to forgive us our sins
A) V10b) we make him a liar

The logic of the above A,C,A breakdown

"C" is the general truth
"A" are the specific levels of "C"
("B's" are how to get back in the truth)

V8b) we deceive ourselves (how? V6b, V10b)
    V6b) we lie, instead of telling the truth
    V10b) we make him a liar by not telling the truth in the eyes of others.

How do get back in fellowship with each other?

V9b) He is faithful and just to forgive our sin. What kind of sin? Lying to each other
V6b) we will be back in fellowship with one another

2nd Set of Similar Phrases: Set "c"

A) V6c) do not the truth
B) V7 the blood of Jesus Christ His son cleanseth us from all sin
C) V8c) the truth is not in us
B) V9 and to cleanse us from all unrighteousness
A) V10c) his word is not in us

V8c) the truth is not in us (why? V6c, V10c)
    V6c) we don't do the truth (we don't live the truth)
    V10c) His word (truth) is not in us. (we have not renewed our mind to hold the truth)

How do get back in fellowship with each other?

B) V7c *the blood of Jesus Christ His son cleanseth us from all sin*
B) V9c *and to cleanse us from all unrighteousness*

If you read them in the outline form, it will add a greater understanding. That is: Read the "A's" together, the "B's" together, and "C" as a center point. Reading them backwards is also interesting where each "C" phrase corresponds to a phrase in each "A" set which I have detailed above.

Please note V7 and V9 (B) are the solution of V8 (C) when you read them like this: C, BB.

Please note that V6 and V10 (A) are reinforcing or showing you the "why" or "how" of V8 (C) when you read them like this: C, AA.

5: That which we heard from the beginning, that we should love one another.

> 1 John 3:11 KJV
> 11 For this is the message that ye heard **from the beginning**, that we should love one another.
>
> 2 John 1:5-6 KJV
> 5 And now I beseech thee, lady, not as though I wrote a new commandment unto thee, but that which we had **from the beginning**, that we love one another.
> 6 And this is love, that we walk after his commandments. This is the commandment, That, as ye have heard **from the beginning**, ye should walk in it.

In the first chapter of this book, I wanted to establish a base understanding of how the phrase **"from the beginning"** is used in the remoter contexts well as the main topics and connected words that revolve around this phrase. At one point I had wanted to see if there was a common thread in the Bible about this phrase. I was not looking for anything specific, but I wanted the context, the story, the principle, the mindset, and any lists that are revealed around this phrase.

As we have seen in Chapter One, Deuteronomy 10-11 where the phrase **"from the beginning"** is used for the first time, has the context of how God has met *(and will meet)* the believer's needs if they follow His Word, that is: as they endeavour to live His Word with an honest heart and soul. This is called "loving God," this is what it is to love God, to do His Word, to live His Word. This involves changing our old ways to live by His new ways, **this is "the renewed mind" principle that God taught to Moses to write down by revelation in the book of Deuteronomy**.

As I continued looking up this phrase, every use was associated with the remoter context of changing our thoughts and actions. That is, to do God's Word, to walk in God's Word, to renew our mind to God's Word. Therefore, during my study, the main topic of this book became clearer, that this book should focus upon how we can change our thoughts and actions so that we can live God's Word in our daily lives. God has always required believers to exercise self-control to receive His blessings **from the beginning.**

> **Deuteronomy 10:12-13 KJV**
> **12 And now, Israel, what doth the LORD thy God require of thee, but to**

fear *(respect)* the LORD thy God, **to walk** in all his ways, and **to love** him, and **to serve** the LORD thy God with all thy heart and with all thy soul,
13 **To keep** the commandments of the LORD, and his statutes, which I command thee this day for thy good?

1. **To respect** the Lord
2. **To walk** in His ways
3. **To love** Him
4. **To serve** the Lord, with **all your heart,** and **all your soul.** That is, with your whole being or life.
5. **To Keep** the commandments of the Lord.

These are all things that are in the "renewed mind" category. These are all choices we make as believers, as Christians, in our daily walk to do God's Word. The phrase **"require of thee"** is the key that tells us **"WE"** are the ones who must **"DO"** these five things listed in Deuteronomy 10:12-13. We must figure out by studying God's Word what is **"required of thee,"** to carry them out. Deuteronomy 11:1 is one example of what we need to do to figure out how to carry out God's Word in our life.

> **Deuteronomy 11:1 KJV**
> 1 Therefore thou shalt **love** the LORD thy God, and **keep** ¹his charge, and

(keep) ²**his statutes,** and *(keep)* ³**his judgments,** and *(keep)* ⁴**his commandments, alway.**

The Hebrew word translated **"keep"** in Deuteronomy 11:1 has a unique role in this verse. It is utilizing at least two figures of speech. The first one is obvious, as I have supplied the word **"keep"** above.

The figure of speech is called: "The Ellipsis of Repetition" and means: *Where the omitted word or words is, or to be supplied out of a "preceding" or "following" clause, in order to complete the sense.*[37]

I know this because there is another figure of speech of the repetition of the word **"and"** above in a lighter shading. This figure of speech is used to make a list, and to emphasis each thing in the list. The first thing mentioned in this list has the word **"keep"** in it, and in the following three things in the list, we are to supply the word **"keep"** completing the phrase in our understanding.

---

[37] Bullinger, E.W. *(Figures of Speech used in the Bible)*, Baker Book House, Grand Rapids, Michigan.16ᵗʰ printing 1991. p. 70, ref: C. The Ellipsis of Repetitions, simple.

This figure of speech is called: "Polysyndeton" or "many ands." And means: *the repetition of the word "and" at the beginning of successive clauses.*[38]

So, now we know that each of the four things listed starts with the word **"keep."** The word **"keep"** in the Hebrew has five separate definitions, depending on the word that is associated with it in the clause it is used with. This is where this word becomes fascinating to look at. The four associated words in Deuteronomy 11:1 are:

1. **Charge**
2. **Statutes**
3. **Judgements**
4. **Commandments**

Each word above has its own meaning in the Hebrew and will help us determine the correct meaning of the word **"keep"** for each word.

The Hebrew word for the word "keep" is "mishmereth" (H4931) and is pronounced: "mish-meh'-reth" and means: *1) Custody, guard, 2) a keeping, 3) observance, or performance of an office, 4) that which is observed, a law, a rite, 5) to keep on anyone's side.*[39]

---

[38] Ibid., p. 208, ref: Polysyndeton or Many Ands.

[39] Gesenius, H.W.F., *(Genesius' Hebrew-Chaldee Lexicon to the Old Testament)*, Baker Books House Company, Grand Rapids, MI. ©1979. p. 518, ref: 4931, 1-5.

So, with each word in the list of 4 things, the word **"keep"** can have a different meaning of the same Hebrew word. But in this case, there are two pairs of words associated with the word **"keep,"** where **"keep"** uses the same meaning. But, each associated word in the pair has slightly different nuances that would naturally pair them up. One of the words in each pair has a straight forward meaning, while the other word in the pair has a moral or practical sense. I have paired them up below with different shadings along with the slightly different nuances.

1. **#1 Charge** = Definition #3 Observance of performance of an office (ministry), emphasizing the operation of a ministry in a general sense.
2. **#3 Judgements** = Definition #3 Observance of performance of an office but emphasizing the impartial judgement to make the right decision.

3. **#2 Statutes** = Definition #4 That which is observed, a law, a rite. In way of a custom to carry it out.
4. **#4 Commandments** = Definition #4 That which is observed, a law, a rite. This is the law itself.

As you see, **"charge" and "judgements"** are related, but one is a more general meaning, and one is the application of the office in a judicial or moral way.

The same is true for **"statutes" and "commandments."** One is the law itself, and the other is how the law is carried out in a moral way.

What we have are two categories in these four words that are paired up. One pair deals with our calling and that we should carry it out in a judicious way; the other deals with God's Word and making sure we apply it in the right way. These two briefly cover our complete walk as a Christian concerning our renewed mind in practice.

So, the word **"keep"** is to be supplied in front of each clause, and each connected words' definition determines the exact definition and nuance that is used of the same Hebrew word translated **"keep"** to give us a more precise understanding in the four things we are to renew our mind in to love God as Deuteronomy 11:1 lays out.

Now, you will notice that the phrase **"love one another"** and the phrase **"This is love"** in 2nd John 1:5-6 are a common topic of the key verses in this chapter. We are given a command to **"love one another,"** a phrase which is used thirteen times in the Bible. The phrase **"this is love"** is used once in the

Bible and it occurs directly after the last use of the phrase **"love one another"** in 2 John 1:6.

Let's look at the only use of **"this is love"** and see what we are to do that is called "love." There are many philosophies that teach that this love is "being all "Lovey Dovey," towards everyone. **This is not what God's Word teaches.** God's love is bold, honest, direct at times, truthful. But it is also loving, patient, understanding, etc. If someone asked you to define God's love in our lives, could you give an answer? What is God's love as defined by His Word, not what we think it should mean? It is:

- **Keeping His Word by changing our habits to reflect His truth,** His views, the lifestyle that He wants us to live by.
- **Renewing your mind** *(your thoughts, habits)* **to live His Word** in your lifestyle, keeping His commandments. That is walking or living **"in "God's Love."**

2 John 1:6 KJV
6 And this is love, that we walk after his commandments. This is the commandment, That, as ye have heard from the beginning, ye should walk in it.

What is directly after the phrase **"this is love"**?

"**that we walk after His commandments."**
Is this love a feeling?
Is this love an emotion?
Is this love turning the other cheek, or being "lovey-dovey?
NO! This love is a decision to "walk after" or to conduct your walk according to God's Word.
Who does the "regulating of yourself" to live God's Word"?
God or You?

YOU! YOU conduct yourself by renewing your mind to get rid of behaviors that are against God's Word and replace them with behaviors that are in line with God's Word.

You don't ask God to take away those wrong behaviors for you, **YOU** take away those wrong behaviors by **YOU** replacing them with "right" behaviors from God's Word.

We should never blame God for any lack of discipline and self-control on our part. And we should avoid saying, "it must not be God's will" when and if we fall short. Because if there is **ONE VERSE** that tells you that is wrong and not becoming for a believer, it is 2 John 1:16! **IT IS GOD'S WILL** for **US** to change our own behavior to line up with God's Word, and thus live in God's love by way of that new behavior!

There are two more grammatical points I want to bring to your attention concerning a figure of speech of repetition that makes this verse a paragraph on its own before we move on. The repeated word is **"walk,"** used at the beginning and the end of the verse with a very important message in between. And as a second point of interest considering the immediate context, the word after each word **"walk"** adds some real emphasis to the whole concept shared in this verse. The two phrases are: **"walk after,"** and **"walk in."**

The figure of speech of repetition that makes this a paragraph on its own is called: "Epanadiplosis" or "Encircling" and means: *The repetition of the same word or words at the beginning and end of a sentence. It means a doubling upon again...The Latins called it INCLUSIO, inclusion: either because the first word is included at the end, or because of the importance of the matter which is thus included between the two words.*[40]

With this figure of speech, the words that are used in the beginning and end of a sentence are also called **"bookends"**[41] because that is where bookends are placed, boxing in the subject of the verse to draw our

---

[40] Bullinger, E.W. *(Figures of Speech used in the Bible)*, Baker Book House, Grand Rapids, Michigan.16th printing 1991. p. 245, **"Epanadiplosis" or "Encircling"**

[41] Nessle, Jon O., *(Repetitions-Revealing a Hidden Key to the Heart of Scripture)*, Next Reformation Publishing Co. Plainfield, https://www.academia.edu/24932331/

attention to **"what"** we should be **"walking after"** or **"walking in."** That we should **"walk after"** and **"walk in"** *His commandments (used twice) that we have heard from the beginning, which is "to love God first.*

> **Matthew 22:37-38 KJV**
> **37 Jesus said unto him, Thou shalt love the Lord thy God with all thy heart, and with all thy soul, and with all thy mind.** *(will all your understanding, your thoughts, the way you think)*[42]
> **38 This is the first and great commandment.**

There you have it... Love God with everything you've got, WHERE? In all your HEART, SOUL, and MIND! Love God in all parts of your thought and decision-making processes in your mind, in your soul, what makes you, you.

The phrase **"walk after"** means to conduct yourself according to what is written in God's Word. The phrase **"walk in"** means to conduct yourself by what is written in God's Word. These are similar phrases. The clauses between these two phrases tell us what we are to **"walk"** according to, or what to **"walk"** by, which is God's Word.

---

[42] Thayer, Joseph H., *(Thayer's Greek-English Lexicon of the New Testament)*, Baker Books House, Grand Michigan, 24th printing. p. 140, ref: 1271

To love God is to **"walk after"** and **"walk in"** His Word. This is the **RENEWED MIND WALK** in this verse!

So, to love with God's love is to conduct your life to live God's Word. That is: to renew your mind, so you are doing His Word.

When you are living God's Word by renewing your mind, YOU ARE "loving God!"

Let's look at some of the other verses with the phrase **"love one another"** as in 2nd John 1:5. We first needed 2nd John 1:6 to be explained, so we could understand what love is. Then, we could understand the second great commandment that also included the "love" that Jesus Christ mentioned to the Pharisees.

> **Matthew 22:39-40 KJV**
> **39 And the second** *is* **like unto it, Thou shalt love thy neighbour as thyself.**
> **40 On these two commandments hang all the law and the prophets.**

The phrase **"love one another"** is used thirteen times in twelve verses. The first and second use are in the first verse the phrase is used in. And this verse will help set the base meaning beyond the raw definition from the Greek dictionary. This first and second use will enlighten us.

John 13:34 KJV
34 A new commandment I give unto you, That ye love one another; as I have loved you, that ye also love one another.

First, the general subject is that Jesus Christ is our example on how to love one another. Secondly, he is giving us a new command *(charge)* to love one another as he has loved us. Do you see the repetition "encircling" or "bookends?" Do you see the clause in between the repeated phrase that tells us HOW to love one another? How do we **"love one another"** according to phrase inside the repetition? **We love one another as Jesus Christ loves us, that how!** This is the main subject in this verse because of the repetition "encircling."[43, 44]

The context surrounding this phrase, not only in this verse, but others will show us a "connected" context that will add more understanding for us, so we can apply this love in our life.

It really is something how God's Word keeps us on track, if we take the time to slow down and work the

---

[43] Bullinger, E.W. *(Figures of Speech used in the Bible)*, Baker Book House, Grand Rapids, Michigan.16th printing 1991. p. 245, **"Epanadiplosis" or "Encircling"**

[44] Nessle, Jon O., *(Repetitions-Revealing a Hidden Key to the Heart of Scripture)*, Next Reformation Publishing Co. Plainfield, https://www.academia.edu/24932331/

surrounding context a bit so we can see the subjects or topics that are connected in a broader way to what we are studying. This keeps us honest when we study. We let God's Word show us the connections; not the other way around. We don't go to God's Word with our preconceived connections and isolate verses that may confirm our theology if we "twist" the meaning just a little.

John 13:35 KJV
35 By this shall all *men* <u>know</u> that ye are my <u>disciples</u>, if ye have love one to another.

"By this:" what are these two words referring to? Loving others with the same love Jesus Christ loved us with from John 13:34. When others see this love in your life towards others, they will **"know"** *(learn to know)*[45] that you are a **"disciple"** *(pupil)*[46] of Jesus Christ. When you are a pupil, you're learning to apply the teachings from your teacher. You're changing your habits to be like your teacher, you're renewing your mind to live his teachings. In this instance, to live with the same love he loved you with. So, others will learn to know that you are a

---

[45] Meyers, Rick, (*Thayer's Greek Lexicon Dictionary*) E-Sword Software Version 11.1.0, Copyright ©2000-2017. **ginōskō**, ref: G1097, verb, *1) to learn to know, come to know, get a knowledge of perceive, feel.*

[46] Ibid., **mathētēs**, ref: G3101, noun, *1) a learner, pupil, disciple.*

follower of Jesus Christ because of the love have toward them.

The next verse with the phrase **"love one another"** is John 15:12, which is a condensed version of John 13:34. And the immediate context is more obvious than the last verse. I will quote the related verses, so you can see it also.

> **John 15:9-14 KJV**
> ➡ 9 As the Father hath loved me, so have I loved you: continue ye in my love.
> ➡ 10 If ye keep my commandments, ye shall abide in my love; even as I have kept my Father's commandments, and abide in his love.
> 11 These things have I spoken unto you, that my joy might remain in you, and *that* your joy might be full.
> ➡ 12 This is my commandment, That ye love one another, as I have loved you.
> 13 Greater love hath no man than this, that a man lay down his life for his friends.
> 14 Ye are my friends, if ye do whatsoever I command you.

There is a lot to unpack in these verses, but I have highlighted what is pertinent to our study. John 15:12 is where the phrase **"love one another"** is used, but John 15:9-14 shows us the surrounding context and it looks like we have a cluster of one word or several forms of a root word. This makes it a repetition, and being a cluster, places some importance on the repeated words as a major topic in a larger section. The repeated word is **"command (ment (s))**," So we should look at the phrases these related words are used in.

1. V9: "**continue you** in my love"
2. V10: "**if you keep** my commandments," "**keep** my Fathers commandments"
3. V12: "**this is my commandment**" that you love one another as I have loved you.
4. V14: "**if you do** whatsoever I command you"

All four phrases charge us to ACT on these commandments. One of the four phrases (John 15:9) charge us to **"continue"** in his love, which is his command in the immediate context. John 15:12 is the pivotal verse, and complements John 15:9. The main topic is to love as God has loved Jesus Christ, and how Jesus Christ loved us, and how we are to love in the same way.

> **John 15:9, 12 KJV**
> **9 As the Father hath loved me, so have I loved you: continue ye in my love.**
> **12 This is my commandment, That ye love one another, as I have loved you.**

How? By **keeping** or **doing His commandments** that we have been charged to do by Jesus Christ. In John 15:10 the word **"if"** is the key that tells us **WE** are the ones who must carry out the command to love one another as Jesus Christ loved us. Just as an employee has a choice to carry out their bosses' charge to do a task for them. **"If"** the employee refuses to, by their freedom of will to carry it out, they can lose their job. **"If"** we decide not to carry out the charge to **"love one another"** from Jesus Christ, we will lose the blessings that were associated with it.

Words like **"if," "let," "beseech,"** are all signals to us as we read God's Word of actions we need to carry out through our freedom of will to obey God's Word. It is always a choice between God's way or our own way. This is the renewed mind in action. By doing God's Word, we are loving God!

The next verse we will look at is not the next in order, and the skipped verses do have different topics related to our phrase. But the one I want to share is quite unique in what it says, and in the context in the verse. Read this verse a few times to bring it all in! I have referenced the Greek in parentheses in the footnotes. This verse tells us that as we change our bad habits to godly habits, our mind is literally healed from those bad habits that are against God and His word, and our godly love grows.

1 Peter 1:22 KJV
22 Seeing ye have purified *(morally cleansed)*[47] **your souls** *(the seat of your personal life, your heart, desires)*[48] **in obeying the truth** ~~through the Spirit (omitted in all major critical Greek texts)~~[49] **unto** *(moving towards)*[50] **unfeigned love of the brethren,** *see that ye* love one another **with a pure heart fervently:**

I have corrected the above verse, taking out the added words from the translators and with Greek meanings of some of the words I replaced with the parentheses.

1 Peter 1:22 KJV
22 Seeing ye have *(morally cleansed)* **your** *(seat of your personal life)* **in obeying the truth unto** *(moving towards)* **unfeigned**

---

[47] Meyers, Rick, (*Thayer's Greek Lexicon Dictionary*) E-Sword Software Version 11.1.0, Copyright ©2000-2017 **hagnizō** G48, *1) ceremonially, 1a) to make pure, purify, cleanse,* **2) morally** (I believe as we renew our mind, our morals will also change)

[48] Ibid., **psuchē** G5590, *2) the soul 2a) the seat of the feelings, desires, affections, aversions (our heart, soul etc.)*

[49] Wierwille, V.P., *(Receiving the holy spirit today),* American Christian Press, New Knoxville, Ohio 1982. p. 234: B, p. 291 ref: 1st Peter 1:22: *... obeying the truth unto unfeigned love of the brethren...*

[50] Thayer, Joseph H., *(Thayer's Greek-English Lexicon of the New Testament),* Baker Books House, Grand Michigan, 24th printing. p. 184, ref: B used metaphorically: *I) retains the force of entering in anything. 1) where one thing is said to be changed into another...* (our unloving ways are changed to loving ways as we replace our bad habits with godly habits)

love of the brethren, *see that ye* **love one another** **with a pure heart fervently:**

If you are "obeying the truth," you are renewing your mind *(thoughts)* to apply *(carry out willingly)* God's Word. One of the benefits is that your morality *(the bad parts)* are being cleansed or purged by changing those habits to good, godly habits. You are literally destroying them by replacing them with godly habits. This is a part of growing our love towards others as Jesus Christ loved us. By living the Word of God, you will grow your love to love as Jesus Christ loved us towards the brethren.

1 John 4:12 KJV
12 No man hath seen God at any time. If we love one another, God dwelleth in us, and his love is perfected in us.

This verse says basically the same thing 1st Peter 1:22 says, just in another way. Again, notice the signal word **"if"** that tells us it is by our freedom of will that we decide to **"love one another"** the same way Jesus Christ loved us. And **"if"** we do this, **then** his love is "perfected" in us. His love is added to us until we love perfectly in his love. That is, we will grow in his love to love as he loves.

The word "perfected" is the Greek word "teleioō" G5048 and is pronounced "tel-i-o'-o" and means: *2)* *to complete (perfect), i.e. add what is yet wanting in order to render a thing full.*[51]

There are four categories that become known as you look up the uses of the word "perfected" from the Greek.

1. Jesus Christ "completing" his calling.
2. A believer "completing" their work in Christ.
3. God's strength "completed" in us via operating our gift holy spirit.
4. God's love will be made complete in us as we live His Word. (Now, and in the future).

It is with God's gift of holy spirit and our renewed mind that we can love as Jesus Christ loved, no matter what is going on around us.

> **2 Corinthians 12:9 KJV**
> **9 And he said unto me, My grace is sufficient for thee: for my strength is made perfect in weakness. Most gladly therefore will I rather glory in my infirmities, that the power of Christ may rest upon me.**
> **1 John 4:12-17 KJV**
> **12 No man hath seen God at any time. If we love one another, God dwelleth in us, and his love is perfected in us.**

---

[51] Ibid., Thayer, Joseph, H. p. 618, ref: 5048, def: 2

13 Hereby know we that we **dwell** in him, and he in us, because he hath given us of his Spirit.

14 And we have seen and do testify that the Father sent the Son *to be* the Saviour of the world.

15 Whosoever shall confess that Jesus is the Son of God, God **dwelleth** in him, and he in God.

16 And we have known and believed the love that God hath to us. God is love; and **he that dwelleth** in love dwelleth in God, and God in him.

17 Herein is our love **made perfect**, that we may have boldness in the day of judgment: because as he is, so are we in this world.

I have underlined another repetition that relates back to our renewed mind in this section. This is a secondary topic of this section and relates to us being made perfect *(complete)* in God's love. The word is **"dwelleth"** and is used three times with a black background above. This is **how** we stay in fellowship and continue in living God's Word, as we love God by renewing our mind. This section will help show us that making use of our gift holy of spirit and renewing our mind are mentioned as to what we need to do have God's love perfected *(completed)* in us.

- V13-14: Because we have His gift holy spirit, we know we can continue in Him, and He in us. This is the proof that Jesus Christ is the savior. *(this implies we are utilizing our gift holy spirit; we are manifesting it).*
- V15: To confess Jesus Christ is bigger than getting born-again. For God to continue in us, and us to continue in God we must be living His Word. *(This is by the renewed mind)*
- V16: To know and believe God's love is to act and live within God's Word. Therefore, you know and believe that you are "in-Him," and He is "in-you." *(This is by the renewed mind)*
- V17: Therefore, His love is completed in you (V13-14, 15, 16)

The word is "dwelleth" is the Greek verb "menō" (G3306) and is pronounced "men'-o" and is the verb form and means: *To continue, to remain. (In reference to time): To continue to be, to live.*[52]

---

[52] Meyers, Rick, (*Thayer's Greek Lexicon Dictionary*) E-Sword Software Version 11.1.0, Copyright ©2000-2017. Ref: G3306, General, and In reference to time/person.

6: How to apply God's Word: The renewed mind: Key Words

> Romans 12:2 KJV
> 2 And be not conformed to this world: but be ye transformed by the renewing of your mind, that ye may prove what *is* that good, and acceptable, and perfect, will of God.

This chapter will deal with verses that have key phrases or words that indicate it is our responsibility to change our actions, words or phrases such as "put on," "put off," "I beseech you," "if," "let," or phrases that indicate "our choice" to do something, like the shaded phrases above for instance. I will put each study in a separate sub-chapter as a sub-topic, so you can read about each word or phrase as one study.

Throughout the Epistles Paul and others have encouraged the believers under their leadership to actively replace their habits that are contrary to God's Word and Christian living with habits that conform to God's Word and promote unity in the one body of Christ. Some of the bad habits are: lying, envy, jealousy, backbiting, speaking evil against others, cheating on your spouse, causing strive on purpose to cause division, all of which lead to a similar result within the one body of Christ, to divide the unity and collective like-mindedness of their believing and camaraderie.

This kind of division will cause the believers not to live the bigger goal in which the family of God works together like a well-oiled machine with all the believers contributing to the building up of their fellow believers among each other. The dynamic renewed mind for each believer is the key to live in harmony and in balance within the one body of Christ, the family of God. Then, each believer will be operating their gift of holy spirit along with their natural talents to build up and bless the family of believers in their area.

6a: PUT ON

The first phrase we will look at is the phrase **"put on."** There are three categories this phrase is used with: two of the three are controlled by our actions, one is controlled by Jesus Christ at His return. #1 affects our outward surroundings, #2 affects our spiritual continuance, #3 affects our actions through changing our thoughts. And this use will naturally fall in category #3 listed below. I will show you in a little bit some verses where "put on" used for each category.

1. Putting on something, like clothing
   a. *affects our outward surroundings*
2. Putting on our new spiritual body
   a. *affects our spiritual continuance*
3. Putting on the renewed mind
   a. *affects our actions through changing our thoughts.*

Colossians 3:5-17 KJV
5 *(You)* **Mortify** therefore your members which are upon the earth; *(you mortify)* fornication, *(you mortify)* uncleanness, *(you mortify)* inordinate affection, *(you mortify)* evil concupiscence, and *(you mortify)* covetousness, which is idolatry:
6 For which things' sake *(the above list)* the wrath of God cometh on the children of disobedience:
7 In the which ye also walked *(in, at)* some time, when ye lived in them.
8 But now **ye also put off** all these; anger, *(you put off)* wrath, *(you put off)* malice, *(you put off)* blasphemy, *(you put off)* filthy communication out of your mouth.
9 *(You)* **Lie not** one to another, seeing that **ye have put off** the old man with his deeds;
10 And *(you)* **have put on** the new *man*, which is renewed in knowledge after the image of him that created him:

11 Where there is neither Greek nor Jew, circumcision nor uncircumcision, Barbarian, Scythian, bond *nor* free: but Christ *is* all, and in all.

12 *(You)* **Put on** therefore, *(because we are one body in Christ -V11)* **as the elect of God, holy and beloved,** *(you put on)* **bowels of mercies,** *(you put on)* **kindness,** *(you put on)* **humbleness of mind,** *(you put on)* **meekness,** *(you put on)* **longsuffering;**

13 *(You put on)* **Forbearing one another, and forgiving one another, if any man have a quarrel against any: even as Christ forgave you,** **so also** *do* **ye.**

14 **And above all these things** ~~put on~~ *(you put on)* **charity, which is the bond of perfectness.**

15 **And** *(you)* **let the peace of God rule in your hearts,** *(in a horizontal way, towards others),* **to the which also ye are called in one body; and** **be ye** **thankful.**

16 *(You)* **Let the word of Christ dwell in you richly in all wisdom; teaching and admonishing one another in psalms and hymns and spiritual songs, singing with grace in your hearts to the Lord.**

17 **And** **whatsoever ye do** **in word or deed,** *(you)* *do* **all in the name of the Lord Jesus, giving thanks to God and the Father by him.**

You have noticed that I have added some phrases in the above verses. These added phrases are what is understood in the context of what is written to the believers. Phrases like **"put on," "you put off," "you mortify," "let," "so also do ye," "whatsoever ye do," "you do,"** and **"be ye"** are all in the context of things **we are to do** by changing your actions by changing your thoughts. Therefore, I have added the phrases **"you," "you put on," "you mortify," "you put off," "you do,"** that are understood within the context of these verses to bring out the truth in a more direct way. You will notice that we can make a list of things that we are encouraged to change and/or do that will involve changing our thinking and our corresponding actions.

> *The main emphasis in this section is that we are the ones who are responsible to do the right thing by changing our minds and doing what is suggested so we can live in harmony with all the believers because the peace from God is shed abroad in us. Because we are a part of the "one body in Christ" regardless of any doctrinal differences other born-again believers may have. And we are to be thankful to God in the name of Jesus Christ.*

So, what are the areas Paul is pointing out that we should make every effort to put on in our lives? We can live with all the believers, considering we are all a part of the one body in Christ *(if we have God's gift of holy spirit in each of us)* even if there are doctrinal differences, and various stages of understanding, because these are our brothers and sisters in Christ. We all need to be reminded that God has set all the members of the one body of Christ as it has pleased Him, and not just in your church. They all have a purpose to win those that are lost to God in a way we could never reach.[53] In 1st Corinthians 12:12-27 Paul gives more detail on this topic of the "one body" in Christ.

Here are the areas that Paul is listing in this section for the believers to either stop *(put off)*, or to do *(put on)*.

God will not take away *these habits or attitudes from us.* **This section is very clear on this matter, we are the ones who control our thoughts and actions and we are the ones who must stop any of them that are listed in this section.**

Stop "praying" for God to take away your lying.... Just stop lying by telling the truth!

Stop "praying" for God to take away your anger... Just stop being angry in excess!

---

[53] 1 Corinthians 12:18 KJV
18 But now hath God set the members every one of them in the body, as it hath pleased him.

Stop praying for God to take away your wrath ... Just stop letting things build up to point of lashing out with anger!

Don't blame God for your lack of character and commitment to change or stop your corrupt habits. By saying things like "it must not be God's Will." You just read God's Will! Now you change your life to match God's Will!

You *are* saved by grace, but you still have your old mind that has not yet changed to live God's Will. That is your job to change your old corrupt habits, not God's. God already did His part to save you and give His gift of holy spirit. Now, it is your turn to answer His calling, just as Saul did after he was confronted by the resurrected Christ. It took some time to get his thinking right with God. *(Acts 9:1-19, he was with the believers for "certain days" where he was no doubt learning about being a Christian and renewing his mind (thoughts and actions).*

Actions <u>we are to stop</u> by our freedom of will: "mortify," or "put off."

1. fornication,
2. uncleanness,
3. inordinate affection,
4. evil concupiscence,
5. covetousness, which is idolatry:

6. anger, *(instant anger, emotional anger)*
7. wrath, *(anger after a period that is built up and then released)*
8. malice,
9. blasphemy,
10. filthy communication out of your mouth.
11. lie not one to another,

Actions we are to put on by our freedom of will that will replace the actions we are putting off from the list above.

1. bowels of mercies,
2. kindness,
3. humbleness of mind,
4. meekness,
5. longsuffering;
6. forbearing one another,
7. forgiving one another,
8. love with God's love
9. let the peace of God rule in your hearts,
10. be ye thankful.
11. let the word of Christ dwell in you richly
    a. in all wisdom;
    b. teaching and admonishing one another in psalms
    c. and hymns
    d. and spiritual songs,
    e. singing with grace in your hearts to the Lord.

12. whatsoever ye do in word or deed,
    a. *do* all in the name of the Lord Jesus,
    b. giving thanks to God and the Father by him.

I believe verses 10-11 of Colossians 3 are the main subject of this section. Verses 10-11 sum up the two main points that are detailed in the balance of the section, the renewed mind *(verse 10)* and the one body in relation to renewed mind *(verse 11 in essence)*. To see the "one body," the mystery to live, we need to change our way of thinking along with our corresponding actions to line up with God's Word.

> **Colossians 3:10-11**
> **10 And have put on the new *man*, which is renewed in knowledge after the image of him that created him:**
> **11 Where there is neither Greek nor Jew, circumcision nor uncircumcision, Barbarian, Scythian, bond *nor* free: but Christ *is* all, and in all.**

In the renewed mind, we see that it does not matter what country you are from, or what religion you were in the past. All that matters now is that we have Christ in us, and therefore, we are all a part of the one body of Christ. We are to renew our minds according to what God has given us in Christ, in the gift of holy spirit. Christ is in us, and we are now members in particular in that one body.[54]

The renewed mind will allow us to see how the collective body of Christ works, to make sure all the believers are getting their needs met. This is done by those who are working their long suits in a favorable environment of believing to see to it that the believers are getting built up as a part of the family of God. Even a church that may not excel in knowledge has a place in the "one body" and is contributing to the one body in Christ. We should not look down on them or belittle them, for whom Christ lived, died, and rose from dead, and has given them the same gift we have! They are a part of the same "one body of Christ" that we are also a part of.

> **Romans 13:12-14 KJV**
> **12 The night is far spent, the day is at hand: <u>let us</u> therefore cast off the works of darkness, and <u>let us</u> put on the armour of light.**
> **13 <u>Let us</u> walk honestly, as in the day; not in rioting and drunkenness, not in chambering and wantonness, not in strife and envying.**

---

[54] Ephesians 4:4 KJV
4 *There is* one body, and one Spirit, even as ye are called in one hope of your calling;

14 But put ye on the Lord Jesus Christ, and make not provision for the flesh, to fulfil the lusts thereof.

There are two categories above about the renewed mind. There are two contrasting thought processes.

1. **Casting off the works of darkness** *how*? Make no provisions for the flesh.
2. **Putting on the armour of Light** *how*? Walking honestly in the Lord Jesus Christ.

There are some phrases that remind us we are the ones who are responsible: **"cast off"** or **"put on."** These phrases **"let us"** *(used three times)* is not in the Greek but is understood and properly supplied because of the context: **"let us"** is inserted three times. Here is the KJV without the added phrases.

> **Romans 13:12-13 KJV**
> **12 The night is far spent, the day is at hand:** ~~let us~~ **therefore cast off the works of darkness, and** ~~let us~~ **put on the armour of light.**
> **13** ~~Let us~~ **walk honestly, as in the day; not in rioting and drunkenness, not in chambering and wantonness, not in strife and envying.**

Many times, in Greek grammar, because of the syntax and context, the Greek reader would understand what is understood, so when it comes to translating the Greek into another language, the translator will need to supply the understood words so there is a proper grammatical flow in the other language.

"**Put ye**" in the Greek is used once. "**Make not**" in the Greek is used once. It is obvious that those that are to do the action are "**us**" and "**ye**" and it is understood that the phrase "**make not**" is referring to the "**us**" or "**ye**" in the context. Paul is teaching the believers in Rome that they are the ones responsible to change their corrupt habits and replace them with the good habits reflecting God's love as Jesus Christ walked.

Let's look at a few key words to gain a fuller understanding from the Greek. In the Greek, the words translated "therefore" and "put on" don't have "let us" added in the front, except here.

In Roman 13:12a. "let us therefore" is one Greek word "oun" G3767 and is pronounced "oon" and means: *1) then, therefore, **accordingly, consequently**, these things being so.*[55]

In Romans 13:12b. "let us put on" is the one Greek word "enduo" G1746 and is pronounced "en-doo'-

---

[55] Meyers, Rick, *(Thayer's Greek Lexicon Dictionary)* E-Sword Software Version 11.1.0, Copyright ©2000-2017. Ref: 3767

o" and means: *1) to sink into (clothing), put on,* **clothe one's self.**[56]

> **Romans 13:12 KJV**
> **12 The night is far spent, the day is at hand:** ~~let us therefore~~ *[accordingly]* **cast off the works of darkness, and** ~~let us put on~~ *[cloth yourself with]* **the armour of light.**

> **Romans 13:12** *corrected for the 2 Greek words above.*
> **12 The night is far spent, the day is at hand: <u>accordingly</u> cast off the works of darkness, and <u>cloth yourself with</u> the armour of light.**

As you read the above verse with a better translation from the Greek, you can quickly see that the ones who "cast off" or "cloth yourself with" are the individuals Paul is talking to. So, the "let us" in the original translation has plausibility.

When you get dressed, do you put on all your clothes at once? No, you start with the foundation, you put on your under garments, then you put on your outer garments that the public will see. Then, you put on your shoes or footwear last. This takes time, and you can only put on one piece of clothing at a time, until

---

[56] Ibid: Meyers, Rick, *(Thayer's Greek Lexicon Dictionary),* Ref: 1746

you are completely dressed. Notice we are "dressed in the Armour of light." Armour is something you put on one piece at a time, and in ancient times, one had a servant help with dressing - it could take an hour or so depending upon the complexity of the armour. Point being, the renewed mind takes time, and you work on one thing at a time until you are done.

Of course, we will never have a perfectly renewed mind until we receive our new spiritual body along with our new mind and new powers at the return of Jesus Christ.

> **1 Corinthians 13:9-11 KJV**
> **9** For we <u>know in part</u>, and <u>we prophesy in part.</u>
> **10** But when that which is perfect is come, then <u>that which is in part shall be done away.</u>
> **11** When I was a child, I spake as a child, I understood as a child, I thought as a child: but when I became a man, <u>I put away childish things.</u>

- We have knowledge **in part**, which includes God's Word and revelation, so the most renewed mind we can have is still **in part, limited.**

- Our gift of holy spirit is **in part**, it is a token, a down payment, no matter how proficient we are in utilizing the power in our gift of holy spirit, we only operate that power **in part, with limits.**
- Our physical body is temporary before the return of Jesus Christ, it is also **in part, limited.**

When we are gathered together at the return of Jesus Christ, we receive all three areas **in full!**

- **Knowledge in full, - all new knowledge -** *(includes a perfectly renewed mind in our current understanding. Includes the full knowledge of the spiritual laws of physics that is unknown right now and surpasses our physical laws of physics that are limited).*
- **Spiritual power in full,** our gift of holy spirit is only a small taste of the full spiritual power we will receive.
- **Spiritual body in full,** with the ability to change what you look like, as Jesus Christ did in his resurrected new spiritual body. The ability and power to travel anywhere in the universe and back in a split second. *(using the laws of physics for the spiritual realm, not the physical realm, which are limited).*

This is our hope, but right now we should make every effort to put on God's Word to help the believers and others that we are around. This is our choice, by our freedom of will. This will guarantee we grow in God's love as we put on God's Word.

6b: LET US

The next phrase we will look at is **"Let us"** as supplied in the King James Version. This phrase has the understood meaning of being a request, or to be encouraged to do something. Like saying to someone, "let's all go to the ball game." This is a request for all of us to do something, that is, to go to the ball game. This phrase is similar, it will, within the clause it sits in, tell what we are requested to do.

> **Galatians 5:25 KJV**
> **25 If we live** *(have life)*[57] **in the Spirit,** *(then)* **let us also walk in the Spirit.**

"If" we have spiritual life because of our gift of holy spirit, **"then"** let us also direct or order our life by walking in that gift of holy spirit.

This verse shows us what **"our will"** should be towards living by God's Word. This is one of those

---

[57] Meyers, Rick, (*Thayer's Greek Lexicon Dictionary*) E-Sword Software Version 11.1.0, Copyright ©2000-2017. **G2198 "zaō"** *1) to live, breathe, be among the living (not lifeless, not dead)*. Hence, I use *"have life"* in the above understanding.

"**if**" and "**then**" verses that is plain and simple in understanding.

We do this by renewing our mind, that is; changing our thoughts which in turn will help change our actions to live God's Word. Renewing our mind is not just changing our bad habits to godly habits, but also learning how to utilize the power we have been given to bless the one body of Christ.

> **Galatians 6:9-10 KJV**
> **9 And let us not be weary in well doing: for in due season we shall reap, if we faint not.**
> **10 As we have therefore opportunity, let us do good unto all** *men*, **especially unto them who are of the household of faith.**

Again, we see our freedom of will, or willingness to follow through with the encouragement in these verses. We decide to "not be weary" or get exhausted from our well doing. Instead of getting weary in well doing, we know that we will be rewarded after the return of Christ for good deeds. So, as we have opportunities, we do good unto all, and especially to the those in household of faith, the family of God, those who a part of the one body of Christ. Our priority is to serve and bless the believers, those who are born-again, regardless of what church or fellowship they attend. If they are born-again, God has chosen them also, and they are a part, a member in particular, of the one body of Christ, a part of the household of faith!

> **Philippians 3:12-17 KJV**
> **12 Not as though I had already attained, either were already perfect:** *(talking about the gathering together)* **but I follow after,** *(pursue, to seek after)* [58] *[the gathering together]* **if that I may apprehend that for which also I am apprehended of Christ Jesus.**
> **13 Brethren, I count not myself to have apprehended:** *(the gathering together)* **but *this* one thing *I do*, forgetting those things which are behind, and reaching forth unto those things which are before,**
> **14 I press toward the mark for the prize of the high calling of God in Christ Jesus.** *(the gathering together)*
> **15 Let us therefore, as many as be perfect, be thus minded: and if in any thing ye be otherwise minded, God shall reveal even this unto you.**

---

[58] Meyers, Rick, (*Thayer's Greek Lexicon Dictionary*) E-Sword Software Version 11.1.0, Copyright ©2000-2017. diōkō G1377, 5) *metaphorically, to pursue 5a) to seek after eagerly, earnestly endeavor to acquire.*

16 Nevertheless, whereto we have already attained, let us walk by the same rule, let us mind the same thing.
17 Brethren, be followers together of me, and mark them which walk so as ye have us for an ensample.

These verses have some great keys we can use to help us renew our minds, so that we can live God's Word as a part of the one body of Christ. In the context, Paul is sharing about how he can boast more than them concerning his past and that he was a person with untouchable credentials and reputation in the high society sector. But he counted all that as waste matter compared to walking in the power of the resurrected Christ. Paul renews his mind and does everything he can to help the believers grow with the anticipation of the gathering together as our final goal to reach. Paul shares in these verses what the believers must do so they too can walk in the power of the resurrection of Christ.

1. V13a: **Forgetting those things in the past** that were not godly (your pre-Christian life)
2. V13b: **Stretch out towards the prize** - our rewards for living God's Word.
3. V14: **Eagerly pursuing the goal** of the gathering together, keep the hope in the forefront of your mind.

4. V16b: **Walk by the same rule, or measure.** (God's Word)
5. V16c: **Think the same thing** (the precepts of God's Word)
6. V17a: **Follow Paul's example**
7. V17b: **Mark believers in your area as an example to follow.**

The above list of attitudes and actions is a fantastic way to support a healthy psychological perspective. Paul is teaching us that we need to move on with our lives and have a goal we can reach for. He is teaching us to forget our past that will prevent us from growing and changing if we dwell on it, and/or makes us feel guilty. He is teaching us to have some people we can look up to and emulate as examples of who we want to be like. Paul is teaching us to order our life with godly practices and principles.

This is all part of **"how"** to renew our mind, **"how"** to change what we think and act on, **"how"** to put God's Word into practice. God allows you to make choices in life, God will never bypass your freedom of will to change you, but God will give us a choice with its benefits, and a choice that has consequences. And we will make a choice one way or the other way.

God will honor your choice along with the consequences it brings. For God to be just, He must allow good and evil to fall on the just and unjust,

our freedom of will along with our choices will help determine the outcome. The outcome could be immediate or take a lifetime to catch up. Look at Adam's first choice that God gave him.

> **Genesis 2:16-17 KJV**
> **16 And the LORD God commanded the man, saying, Of every tree of the garden thou mayest freely eat:**
> **17 But of the tree of the knowledge of good and evil, thou shalt not eat of it: for in the day that thou eatest thereof thou shalt surely die.**

Here was Adam's choice from God, if he obeyed V17, the second part of his choice by not eating from the tree of knowledge of good and evil, Adam's spiritual connection with God would remain with Adam. Adam would continue to have spiritual life from God. If Adam decided to eat of the tree of knowledge of good and evil, Adam would lose his spiritual connection with God. In man's viewpoint, it would die, no longer exist.

> *God has always given man a choice to live by the knowledge of His Word (good), or to live under some other knowledge (evil, the knowledge/schemes from this world)* ***from the beginning****. This is the first choice God gave mankind **in the beginning** of modern mankind.*

Adam had the freedom of will to make his choice, and God would honor whatever choice Adam made. V16 gave Adam information that he could eat of every tree in the garden, and he further was told that one tree would cause him to lose the spirit that God had given him. It was God giving Adam his freedom of will to make his own choice after he had the facts. God would not force Adam one way or the other.

> *God would not take away the tree of knowledge of good and evil for Adam, Adam had to control his mind and actions to obey God's Word. If Adam decided to eat of that tree, then he knew the consequences that God had told him.*

Hebrews 10:26 KJV
26 For if we sin wilfully after that we have received the knowledge of the truth, there remaineth no more sacrifice for sins,

After you have the knowledge of both choices, and you decide to do the wrong choice, you will receive the consequences of that wrong choice, either in this life *(immediately or over time)*, or later when the rewards are handed out for obeying God's Word *(good knowledge)* over man's word *(evil knowledge)*.

There is no way to fix it after you act on the wrong choice. You will not receive any rewards for wrong choices after the gathering together, that is, if you would have made the right choice in the first place, later you would have received a reward. This assumes that you did not renew your choice after you finally "saw the light." If you do change your mind and reverse your choice, the past consequences, if they were not immediate, could change and you would receive a reward for the new choice you made. Adam experienced the consequence of his wrong decision instantaneously and lost his connection with God, so Adam could not fix the consequences.

But God made Adam a promise on how to fix it in the future. In the meantime, they had to live without God's spirit until "the promised seed" came to pass. God did put His spirit on some believers with a limited capacity to make sure His promise would come to pass.

Within the word study in the King James Version of the phrase **"let us"** is a list of lifestyle changes and attitudes we are encouraged to live by, so we can grow in God's love and be a participating member of the one body of Christ. These are not all of them, but most of them.

1. Cast off the works of darkness *(Rom 13:12)*
2. Put on the armour of light *(Rom 13:12)*
3. Walk honestly *(Rom 13:13)*
4. Don't judge one another *(Rom 14:13)*

5. Follow after things which make peace *(Rom 14:19)*
6. Follow after things that build up each other *(Rom 14:19)*
7. Walk in the spirit in operation *(Gal 5:25)*
8. Don't be desirous of vain glory *(Gal 5:26)*
9. Don't get weary in well doing *(Gal 6:9)*
10. Do good unto all men, especially those of the household of faith *(Gal 6:10)*
11. Walk by the same principles *(Phil 3:16)*
12. Be of the same understanding on God's Word *(Phil 3:16)*
13. Love in deed and truth *(1st John 3:18)*
14. Love one another with God's love *(1st John 4:7)*
15. Be glad and rejoice *(Rev 19:7)*

Because all of these are in the "let us" category, these are all a choice we can implement in our life. No one else can do this for us. We are the ones who must look at our lives and decide where we need to change and what we need to do to we change. This is all done with our thoughts, our attitudes, our habits that we need to abandon or tweak to be able to live within the precepts of God's Word.

For instance, in number 8 above: **"let us not be desirous of vain glory"** *(Galatians 5:26)* we are not to be eager for empty glory, or act in a conceited way. Empty glory, or acting in a conceited way, is where a person does things to elevate their ego and cleverness in front of others to make themselves look better than others and have pride in themselves. They glory in themselves, not God, and don't produce any fruits from faith *(or by of believing)*.

This is a decision of their mind, of their thoughts, of their attitude. By changing their thoughts, they can change their mind. They would need to start to do things that would help others with an honest heart and have no thoughts of self-glory or self-benefits in these acts of kindness for others. In other words, it is no longer **"all about me"** but it is now **"all about them and their needs."**

6c: BESEECH

Romans 12:1 KJV
1 I beseech **you therefore, brethren, by the mercies of God, <u>that ye present your bodies a living sacrifice</u>, holy, acceptable unto God,** *which is* **your reasonable service.**

Ephesians 4:1-3 KJV
1 I therefore, the prisoner of the Lord, beseech **you <u>that ye walk worthy of the vocation wherewith ye are called</u>,**
2 With all lowliness and meekness, with longsuffering, forbearing one another in love;

3 Endeavouring to keep the unity of the Spirit in the bond of peace.

The word "beseech" in the Greek is "parakaleō" G3870 and is pronounced "par-ak-al-eh'-o" and means: *2) to address, speak to, (call to, call upon), which may be done in the way of exhortation, entreaty, comfort, instruction, etc. 2a)* **to admonish, exhort** *2b)* **to beg** *(implore),* **entreat, beseech** *2b1)* **to strive to appease by entreaty** *2c) to console, to encourage and* **strengthen by consolation***, to comfort 2c1) to receive consolation, be comforted 2d)* **to encourage, strengthen** *2e) exhorting and comforting and encouraging 2f) to instruct, teach*[59]

I have placed the text above in bold to show some of more common meanings of the Greek word. A very common meaning is: **"to lovingly exhort and encourage"** to do what is requested either in the rest of the verse, or in the following verses that will cover a larger topic. If you look at Ephesians 4:2-3, those are the things they are being exhorted to do or apply in their Christian life.

This is more than a request to do something, it is also a heartfelt feeling towards those you are imploring to act on what you are asking them to do. You are trying to give advice or instruction to help improve their lives, not with hostility, but a genuine concern

---

[59] Meyers, Rick, (*Thayer's Greek Lexicon Dictionary*) E-Sword Software Version 11.1.0, Copyright ©2000-2017. **parakaleō** G3870, def: 2, a-f

for their good and welfare. Or you are asking for help from someone that can help you or your situation. Here is good example in the Gospels.

> **Luke 9:37-42 KJV**
> 37 And it came to pass, that on the next day, when they were come down from the hill, much people met him.
> 38 And, behold, a man of the company cried out, saying, <u>Master, I beseech thee, look upon my son: for he is mine only child.</u>
> 39 And, lo, a spirit taketh him, and he suddenly crieth out; and it teareth him that he foameth again, and bruising him hardly departeth from him.
> 40 And I besought thy disciples to cast him out; and they could not.
> 41 And Jesus answering said, O faithless and perverse generation, how long shall I be with you, and suffer you? Bring thy son hither.
> 42 And as he was yet a coming, the devil threw him down, and tare *him*. And Jesus rebuked the unclean spirit, and healed the child, and delivered him again to his father.

Can you hear the father now, his only child that he loves very much? The compassion he must have had for his only son; the passion to see him healed! As he approaches Jesus Christ and implores him to heal his son, was he emotional? Yes. Was he crying? Possibly, he was undeniably trying to have his only child healed. Did the father have a total commitment and act suitably to have his only son healed? Yes.

In my base verses at the beginning of sub-chapter 6c above the underlined phrases are basically saying the same thing in distinct ways. I will be exploring these phrases in a practical way. One of the ways focuses on being totally committed, the other way is to live suitably to the calling God has called you to. In order to live in the fullness of what God has called you for, you will need a total commitment and act suitably to be the best true Christian you can be.

> **Romans 12:1 KJV**
> **1 I beseech you therefore, brethren, by the mercies of God, that ye present your bodies a living sacrifice, holy, acceptable unto God,** *which is* **your reasonable service.**

This chapter in Romans is the groundwork teaching concerning the topic of **"the renewed mind"** on how to **"present your bodies a living sacrifice"** that will set up the foundation for our actions and attitudes that are needed to be a strong committed believer. The first two verses challenge us to be the best we can for God, because of what God has done for us through Jesus Christ. Then, we read a long list of actions and attitudes that we are encouraged to adopt in our lives.

> **Romans 12:3 KJV**
> **3 For I say, through the grace given unto me, to every man that is among you, <u>not to think *of himself* more highly than he ought to think</u>; but to think soberly, according as God hath dealt to every man the measure of faith.**

The very first thing that Paul mentions we as new believers need to do is not get all puffed up with pride because of what God has given us. Every believer has been given the same amount of the gift of holy spirit through believing. Be thankful you have this great power from God, but don't get all "hoity-toity" and brag how you are now going to "kick the devil's ass." Or as some new believers say, "Bring it on Satan, your ass is mine." **NO, don't get puffed up because you now can defeat Satan!**

That prideful attitude will backfire because you are a **green** Christian, a **newbie** in faith and learning how to work the gift of holy spirit effectively. The spirit does have the power to defeat Satan, but your mind is undisciplined in using that power. By making such declarations you are exposing your over confidence and inexperience. Instead rejoice inwardly and show humility outwardly, exercise self-control, curb your urges to be a "hot-shot" and grow in Christ as a new Christian. There will be a time when you can handle fighting in the spiritual realm. Just as a tree doesn't bear quality fruit in the first year, instead, the tree can take 3 years or more to bear quality fruit. Be patient, grow up in Christ and his knowledge by studying God's Word, and grow up spiritually by speaking in tongues much.[60]

If you are going to "present your body" *(present your life)* as a "living sacrifice" *(a life committed to serve God)*, you will need to get rid of your pride you have because of who you are, and the pride you have because of the power you have, *(this is not godly pride, but earthly pride I am talking about)*. This is the first thing Paul requests the new believers to **NOT DO** from their past way of thinking. Maybe it was because they were full of pride because of what high society position they hold in life, or what pedigree their family is from, or how successful they have been and then applying that way of prideful thinking after becoming a new Christian in their Christian attitude and pridefully bragging to kick Satan's ass, as an example. Paul implores the new Christians **NOT** to act with that kind of pride.

---

[60] Arbib, Peter., *(20+ Benefits Speaking in Tongues Has for You)*, Sound Wisdom Publications, Camby, IN. 2018. Ch. 3: Speaking in tongues edifies you and builds you up. Ch. 6: Speaking in tongues strengthens us with might in our inner man.

The next few verses give us some things we can think about that will guide us to having a humble attitude. Basically, you're not the "Lone Ranger" or the only person that can handle spiritual things. But, instead, you are a part of all the believers collectively referred to in God's Word as "the one body." wherein every believer has a function in particular as they grow and learn their long-suits as a Christian. Knowing that you are a part of a larger collective and that you are just as important as the next believer, helps you to keep humble with your abilities.[61]

> **Romans 12:4-5 KJV**
> **4 For as we have <u>many members in one body</u>, and all members have not the same office:**
> **5 So we, <u>being many, are one body in Christ,</u> and every one members one of another.**

What are some of the other things listed in this "principle teaching" that Paul wants us to adapt to and live by?

1. Romans 12:6: **Edify the church** by working your gift holy spirit... The manifestation of prophecy is given as an example.

---

[61] 1st Corinthians 12:12-27

2. Romans 12:7: **Work your ministry** to help build-up the believers.
3. Romans 12:8a: **Encourage** those that need encouragement.
4. Romans 12:8b: If you **give advice**, give it honestly.
5. Romans 12:8c: If you **lead people**, do it earnestly.
6. Romans 12:8d: If you **show mercy** (unmerited favor), do it promptly with a ready mind.
7. Romans 12:9a: **Love with God's love**, being sincere.
8. Romans 12:9b: Dislike evil, **join yourself to that which is upright.**
9. Romans 12:10: **Have a mutual love towards each other,** with brotherly love, honoring and preferring each other.
10. Romans 12:11a: Not slow doing work, **do your job without wasting your bosses time.**
11. Romans 12:11b: Just as you work without wasting time, you should **have a similar zeal to spiritually serve God.**
12. Romans 12:12a: **Rejoicing in hope.**
13. Romans 12:12b: **Patient in distress.**
14. Romans 12:12c: **Continue in prayer.**
15. Romans 12:13a: **To be a partner to the saints needs.**
16. Romans 12:13b: **To seek after eagerly, hospitality.**

These are all things we should want to make up our mind to incorporate in our actions. We do that by replacing our habits that are opposite of the above list with new habits that reflect the above list.

You must confront the obstacle head-on and consciously change your thoughts to "do the right thing."

God *will not* change your thoughts and bad habits for you. If God did, that would go against His very first commandment in Genesis to Adam where God gave Adam the freedom of will to obey or disobey His Word. Once you start putting these above actions into your lifestyle, you will start to see the profit of what God has called you to.

> **Romans 15:30 KJV**
> **30 Now I beseech you, brethren, for the Lord Jesus Christ's sake, and for the love of the Spirit, <u>that ye strive together with me in your prayers to God for me;</u>**

Another thing Paul exhorts us to do is to pray for him, taking this to the next level of understanding: we are encouraged to pray for our leadership as a collective of believers in a local area. They were to **pray for** *(via speaking in tongues)* that **Paul would bless them by teaching God's Word**, teaching them exactly what they needed to hear. And that **his**

journey would be safe from those that do not believe and that **his mistering would be accepted** by the saints, and it is **God's will with joy to go to them**, and that **they will become refreshed** by the Word he would share with them. And **God's peace would be with all of them**. They were to make intercession for Paul as a local group of believers having a similar mindset in their prayers, *(strive together… in prayers)*.

Paul knew that if all the believers prayed for him as a collective or a group with a similar mindset, he would be delivered from those that don't believe, and that God would inspire him what to teach in God's Word so the believers would be blessed. Hence, they can grow in understanding and application of God's Word in their life. This is one of the great benefits of prayer when many believers pray together, *(either in a local prayer group, and/or everyone praying individually, but for a common goal)* with same mindset.

> **Romans 15:29-33 KJV**
> 29 And I am sure that, when I come unto you, I shall come in the fulness of the blessing of the gospel of Christ.
> 30 Now I beseech you, brethren, for the Lord Jesus Christ's sake, and for the love of the Spirit, that ye <u>strive together with me in your prayers</u> to God for me;

31 That I may be <u>delivered from them that do not believe</u> in Judaea; and that my service which I have for Jerusalem may <u>be accepted of the saints;</u>
32 That <u>I may come unto you with joy by the will of God</u>, and <u>may with you be refreshed.</u>
33 Now <u>the God of peace be with you all.</u> Amen.

In the next use of the Greek word translated "I beseech" Paul is encouraging the Corinthians to get like-minded on God's Word and get rid of their divisions. In 1st Corinthians 1:10 Paul shares what the new believers need to do in their local fellowships so there would be no divisions. Verses 10-17 is the main section of the problems they had that Paul was addressing.

> **1 Corinthians 1:10 KJV**
> 10 Now I beseech you, brethren, by the name of our Lord Jesus Christ, that ye all <u>speak the same thing</u>, and that there be <u>no divisions among you</u>; but that ye be <u>perfectly joined together</u> in <u>the same mind and in the same judgment</u>.

Here are the three categories with two sub-categories that Paul wants the Corinthians to work on, so they would have no divisions among them.

Category #1:
Speak the same thing
 Sub-Category #1: No divisions among them

Category #2: and #3
The same mind
The same judgement
 Sub-Category #2: Perfectly joined together

Okay, now I must go into the Greek to show you why I made the above outline the way I did. There is one overwhelming key that tells us the three major points in this verse. The repetition of the word "autos" (G846) in the Greek, translated: "same thing," "same," and "same." There are two clauses, one is connected with "speak the same thing," the other is connected with "the same mind," and "the same judgment." That is why I made the outline above as I did.

The word "same" in the Greek is the word: "autos" G846 and pronounced "ow-tos'" and means: *1) himself, herself, themselves, itself, 2) he, she, it, 3) the same.*[62]

Considering the subjects of the verse, translating this word "same" would make more sense

---

[62] Meyers, Rick, (*Thayer's Greek Lexicon Dictionary*) E-Sword Software Version 11.1.0, Copyright ©2000-2017. **"autos" G846,** def: 1/itself, 2/it, 3/the same.

grammatically for proper English word flow. I mentioned that this is a repetition that determines the main subjects of the verse. The three main subjects are:

1. Speaking
2. Understanding (mind)
3. Opinions (judgment)

We are not talking about doing things the same way, we are talking about the principles and teachings in God's Word, like what Paul taught on the "fellowship of the mystery," or what Paul taught on the "one body of Christ," or on the "proper order of the speaking manifestations" in 1st Corinthians 14:ff. Paul wants them to have "the same" **understanding of God's Word, the same opinion of God's Word being perfectly joined together in this understanding and opinion of God's Word. And to speak** *(profess one and the same thing[63])* **the same doctrines of God's Word AND that there are no divisions among them.** This is carried out by *rightly dividing* God's Word.

The word **"and"** in the last phrase connects the two clauses together (#2 and #3 above), and the logic suggests if the believers are professing "the same

---

[63] Thayer, Joseph H., *(Thayer's Greek-English Lexicon of the New Testament)*, Baker Books House, Grand Michigan, 24th printing. p. 374, ref: 3004 **legō** def: Sec II, 1g, *to profess one and the same thing.*

opinion," **and** "the same understanding as a collective," that is: the same doctrine," "the same Word of God," then: there will be no divisions among them.

These are areas that constrain each believer to apply the teachings of Paul regarding the mystery, the one body. When you read 1st Corinthians 1:11-17, you will see that they were not behaving like they're a part of the one body, but they all had their separate fellowships where they elevated their leader as if they were Christ, or they elevated "their interpretation" of Paul's teachings. Paul was addressing this problem by teaching them what they were doing, and what they needed to do to change so they could get back on track with living God's Word. I would recommend that you read 1st and 2nd Corinthians a few times to fully grasp all the issues.

Paul had to confront and offer the correctional teachings needed for them to adapt and change so they could get back to applying God's Word and seeing God's blessings in their lives. This is "beseeching."

Many times, when we are asked to act and think a certain way, like at work, some of us tend to find a person who can be our example we can imitate so we can eventually be like them. It is always easier to change ourselves when we have an example, a mentor, to observe and consult with, than doing it alone. It is like having a teacher 24/7 in many cases to give us advice and encouragement to keep at it.

> **1 Corinthians 4:16 KJV**
> **16 Wherefore I beseech you, be ye followers of me.**

Here, Paul was asking the Corinthians to have him as an example to be like in their Christian lives. Having someone to aspire to always helps you grow and learn how to apply the things you are being taught. If you look at the Greek word behind the word translated "followers" above, you will find a fuller understanding of imitating others to help you grow.

When studying a word, there will times when you see a concentration of repetitions of the same word and/or a concentration of the word you are studying plus another form of the word. This is God's way of grabbing your attention and showing you *the* most important section this word is used in. Within that section of scripture will be what is the most important advice concerning your word study and will generally carry through where the word is used in other places.

In this case with the Greek word **"parakaleo" G3870, the verb form**, is translated "beseech" in many occurrences and is used 4 times in two verses, and it is translated in 2nd Corinthians 1:4 three ways.

Now let's look at the 2 verses that have multiple uses of these words. They will teach a lot about exhortation and the effects it can have on others. You could say these 2 verses in this section teach why we should exhort and encourage others to do the right thing. Everyone will benefit if it is done right!

> **2 Corinthians 1:4 KJV**
> 4 Who comforteth G3870-v us in all our tribulation, that we may be able to comfort G3870-v them which are in any trouble, by the <u>comfort</u> G3874-n wherewith we ourselves are comforted G3870-v of God.
>
> **2 Corinthians 1:6 KJV**
> 6 And whether we be afflicted, it is for your <u>consolation</u> G3874-n and salvation, which is effectual in the enduring of the same sufferings which we also suffer: or whether we be comforted, G3870-v it is for your <u>consolation</u> G3874-n and salvation.

- 2nd Corinthians 1:4 **"comforteth," "to comfort," and "comforted."**
- 2nd Corinthians 1:6, it **"we be comforted,"**

That is 4 occurrences of the verb form in two verses, which also qualifies as a figure of speech of "Repetition." But there is more, the noun form is repeated in this section and becomes part of the same repetition *(not becoming a second repetition)* **because it is from the same root word our original word study started with.**

The noun form is used 6 times in 2nd Corinthians 1:4-7, making a total of 10 occurrences of these two forms in 2nd Corinthians 1:3-7. The noun form in the Greek is the word **"paraklēsis"** used in these verses. The six uses of the noun form:

- 2nd Corinthians 1:3, **"comfort,"**
- 2nd Corinthians 1:4, 2nd **"comfort,"**
- 2nd Corinthians 1:5, **"consolation,"**
- 2nd Corinthians 1:6-2x **"consolation,"**
- 2nd Corinthians 1:7, **"consolation."**

Here is an outline form to show you where these related words are in the mentioned verses. I will list the verse, and then the number of times the words are used, then Strong's Number, and then the Greek word and last the translated word. I grayed the number of times these words are used in each verse so we can see what verses have multiple occurrences, those verses are the key verses of emphasis controlled by the figure of speech "Repetition."

1. 2ⁿᵈ Cor. 1:3 (1x) **G3874-n, paraklēsis,** "comfort."
2. 2ⁿᵈ Cor. 1:4 (4x) **G3870-v, parakaleō,** (3x) "comforteth," 1ˢᵗ "comfort," "comforted," **G3874-n,** (1x) **paraklēsis,** 2ⁿᵈ "comfort."
3. 2ⁿᵈ Cor. 1:5 (1x) **G3874-n, paraklēsis,** "consolation."
4. 2ⁿᵈ Cor. 1:6 (3x) **G3874-n, paraklēsis,** (2x) 1ˢᵗ and 2ⁿᵈ "consolation," (1x) **G3870-v, parakaleō,** "comfort."
5. 2ⁿᵈ Cor. 1:7 (1x) **G3874-n, paraklēsis,** "consolation."

Notice that 2 verses have multiple occurrences of these words. These are the verses that are emphasized by the figure of speech of "Repetition." That will be 2ⁿᵈ Corinthians 1:4 and 1:6, which we will look at closer as soon as I show you the definition of the figure of speech used in this section.

The two Greek words "parakaleō" and "paraklēsis" form one large repetition called: "Repetitio," or "Repetition" and means: *Repetition of the same words or words irregularly in the same passage.... A word or words are repeated, not in immediate succession, as in Epizeuxis; not at the beginning, middle, or end of sentences; ... not at definite intervals; but frequently in the same passage and* *irregularly* for the sake of emphasizing and calling attention to it. *(the repeated word or words).*[64]

In extension because of further research in the use of this figure of speech, the above definition can be updated slightly to read as the: *Repetition of the same word or words <u>and/or word or words from the same root used</u> irregularly in the same passage or section of scriptures.* ...

I want to give the definition of the verb form of "beseech" again, it is made up of two words that mean: **"to call aside to invoke."**[65] That's why there are so many sub-meanings. The context will help us understand the usage.

The word "beseech" or "comfort" in the Greek is "parakaleō" G3870 and is pronounced "par-ak-al-eh'-o" and means: *2) to address, speak to, (call to, call upon), which may be done in the way of exhortation, entreaty, comfort, instruction, etc.* 2a) **to admonish, exhort** 2b) **to beg** *(implore)*, **entreat, beseech** 2b1) **to strive to appease by entreaty** 2c) *to console, to encourage and* **strengthen by consolation***, to comfort* 2c1) *to receive consolation,* **be comforted** 2d) **to**

---

[64] Bullinger, E.W. *(Figures of Speech used in the Bible)*, Baker Book House, Grand Rapids, Michigan.16th printing 1991. p. 263, **"Repetitio," or "Repetiton."**

[65] G3844 para, "besides," or "near." G2564 kaleō "to call" akin to the base of G2753 keleuō to command or urge on.

encourage, strengthen 2e) *exhorting and comforting and encouraging* 2f) *to instruct, teach.*[66]

Momentarily, we will look at these 2 verses and how it affects us and the ones we comfort through encouragement. But first, we will look a verse that shows us the true source of comfort, encouragement, and consolation.

> **2 Corinthians 1:3 KJV**
> **3 Blessed be God, even the Father of our Lord Jesus Christ, <u>the Father of mercies,</u>** *(compassion)* **and the God of all comfort;**

This verse shows us the true source of all comfort is God, the creator of the heavens and earth. As a Father, He is a Father of compassion. We are His children by birth, we have been given His gift of spirit when we became born-again. As the creator *(of everything, including His family, the one body of Christ)*, He is our source of exhortation, strength, encouragement. Not only through His Word, but also through His leadership in the one body of Christ. This is what Paul was explaining. God comforted Paul, and then he comforted the believers with that comfort, and in turn Paul and the believers had comfort from each other, that all started with God comforting Paul.

---

[66] Meyers, Rick, (*Thayer's Greek Lexicon Dictionary*) E-Sword Software Version 11.1.0, Copyright ©2000-2017. Ref: G3870

> **2 Corinthians 1:4 KJV**
> **4 Who comforteth us in all our tribulation, that we may be able to comfort them which are in any trouble, by the comfort wherewith we ourselves are comforted of God.**

God, who is the God of all comfort, comforts us when we are under pressure, or being afflicted, or in distress or a crisis, so we may able to comfort those in any similar situation by the same comfort we received from God. God can help us keep our cool and help others in a crisis or any situation where there is a bit of turmoil and a calm reaction is needed.

This is the result of having "comfort" in our mind because God is exhorting us to stay strong, and to endure knowing our believing will deliver us, *(this could be through your gift holy spirit, and/or through your local leadership)*. This will bring a calm and level headedness to our thoughts, so we can comfort those around us.

> **2 Corinthians 1:6 KJV**
> **6 And whether we be afflicted, it is for your consolation and salvation, which is effectual in the enduring of the same sufferings which we also suffer: or whether we be comforted, it is for your consolation and salvation.**

This verse gives us a practical and personal look at what 2nd Corinthians 1:4 says. In verse 5 Paul says even though they have afflictions from their adversary the devil, because they preach Christ, God's encouragement is over abundant through Christ. That means they are activating their gift holy spirit to be delivered and blessed as they preached Christ. They turned to God by making use of their gift holy spirit to be comforted and encouraged in times of trouble.

Now verse 6, If Paul is afflicted or troubled, he is also enduring it, so the believers can be encouraged and delivered. Paul did not let a few obstacles stop him from his mission of helping the believers get a better handle on applying God's Word in their lives. He realized that pushing through those obstacles would also deliver him. Even if there were no obstacles, he would still preach Christ to help them be encouraged and delivered. No matter what the adversary threw at them *(the believers)* or not, Paul was determined to make sure the believers were encouraged and delivered. It was still the believer's freedom of will to follow Paul's encouragement, but when they did take Paul's advice, this also encouraged Paul when he saw them getting blessed and delivered, knowing that God would take care of his needs as he took care of the believer's needs. This is the heart of a man or woman of God towards their people; this is true comfort, or encouragement towards the believers.

The six categories the word "beseech" in the Greek is used in.

1. **Commit to living God's Word** *(Romans 12:1)*
2. **Walk worthy of your calling from God** *(Ephesians 4:1-3)*
3. **Strive together in prayer for your leadership** *(Romans 15:30)*
4. **Speak, understand, and judge from the same precepts of God's Word** *(1st Corinthians 1:10)*
5. **Be followers of your faithful leadership** *(1st Corinthians 4:16)*
6. **God will comfort you, you can now comfort others, others can now comfort more people.** *This is imploring others to keep and do God's Word by council in times of affliction (2nd Corinthians 1:4,6)*

6d: WILLING MIND

1 Chronicles 28:9-10 KJV
9 And thou, Solomon my son, know thou the God of thy father, and serve him with a perfect heart and with a willing mind: for the LORD searcheth all hearts, and understandeth all the imaginations of the thoughts: if thou seek him, he will be found of thee; but

<u>if thou forsake him, he will cast thee off for ever.</u>[67]

10 Take heed now; for the LORD hath chosen thee to build an house for the sanctuary: be strong, and do it.

2 Corinthians 8:10-12 KJV
10 And herein I give my advice: for this is expedient for you, who have begun before, not only to do, but also to be forward a year ago.
11 Now therefore perform the doing of it; that as there was a readiness to will, so there may be a performance also out of that which ye have.
12 For if there be first a willing mind, it is accepted according to that a man hath, and not according to that he hath not.

The heart of the renewed mind is right here in these few verses. It revolves around each one of us having a **READY AND WILLING**[68] mind to follow through in applying God's Word in practice in our own lives. Notice that God looks on your heart and intentions, and God looks on what you have, not what you don't have. God looks on the heart of each of us, and that

---

[67] Dotted underline: here is their choice to do God's Word, or not. Notice the subject of this section is about having a willing mind and carrying it out as they promised. We keep and do God's Word by **our** freedom of will.

[68] Clapp, Wayne., *(Ready and Willing)*, Christian Family Fellowship, Tipp City, Ohio. For further reading on "ready and willing."

is what matters to God. If we have made a commitment to do a thing for God, we should be doing it out of a ready and willing heart to serve others first, and not for show in front of others to boast our reputation, or to gain personal profit.

Let's look at these verses more closely and work a few key words together.

> **1 Chronicles 28:9-10 KJV**
> **9 And thou, Solomon my son, know thou the God of thy father, and serve him with a perfect heart and with a willing mind: for the LORD searcheth all hearts, and understandeth all the imaginations of the thoughts: if thou seek him, he will be found of thee; but if thou forsake him, he will cast thee off for ever.**
> **10 Take heed now; for the LORD hath chosen thee to build an house for the sanctuary: be strong, and do it**

1st Chronicles 28:9 has a phrase I highlighted in grey, *"know thou the God of thy father and serve him with a perfect heart and a willing mind."* David was instructing one of his sons, Solomon, that God has chosen him to build the temple that would hold The Ark of the Covenant and be a place of worship for God's people. This is a father's advice to his son, so he can be successful in his calling from God. So here are the first four prerequisites David mentions to Solomon.

1. [A] KNOW God
2. [B] **SERVE God**
3. [A] WITH A PERFECT MIND
4. [B] **WITH A WILLING HEART**

If you noticed I added an [A] and [B] structure to these four things listed. What is structure, you may ask? It is the how the verse has an outline of understanding, in Chapter four, I show in detail the structure of 1st John 1:6-10 and how it works. This is not haphazard in God's Word -- it is a vital part of how God protects His Word from private interpretation. God employed the vocabulary of the language that the man or woman of God knew when they wrote it down, but God also protected His Word by the inclusion of figures of speech, and by inspiring the structure of the sentences as holy men spoke and wrote. So, what does the structure reveal to us in 1st Chronicles 28:9? You need to match up the [A]'s together and the [B]'s together to see the connection. Structures will be like an outline, and can be in other orders like: A,B,C,-A,B,C, or A,B,C,-C,B,A for instance.

[A] **Know** *(to acquire knowledge)*, With a **perfect heart** *(peaceful soul, or understanding)*.

[B] Serve, With a willing mind

How do I know that this is the correct pairing, and not just my guess? I look at the Hebrew and it becomes obvious from the definitions.

The word "know" in verse 1ˢᵗ Chronicles 28:9 is the Hebrew word: "yâdaˈ" (H3045) and pronounced: "yaw-dahˈ" and means in general terms: *to perceive, to acquire knowledge, to be acquainted.*[69]

The Phrase "perfect heart" on 1ˢᵗ Chronicles 28:9 are the Hebrew words: "shâlêm" (H8003), "lêb" (H3820) and can have several meanings, but in general they mean: completely peaceful soul. **"shâlêm"** means in general terms: *1) complete, safe, peaceful, perfect, whole, full, at peace* [70] **"lêb"** means: *1) inner man, mind, will, heart, understanding* [71]

David was sharing with his son Solomon that he would need to get to know God, and to be able to assimilate knowledge from God, he would need a peaceful inner man, a peaceful soul.

---

[69] Gesenius, H.W.F., *(Genesius' Hebrew-Chaldee Lexicon to the Old Testament)*, Baker Books House Company, Grand Rapids, MI. ©1979. p. 333, ref: 3045-main general definition.

[70] Meyers, Rick, *(Brown-Driver-Briggs Hebrew Dictionary)* E-Sword Software Version 11.1.0, Copyright ©2000-2017. Ref: H8003, def 1.

[71] Ibid., Meyers, Rick, Ref: H3820, def: 1

If you want to receive anything from God, you will need to be at peace inwardly.

David was teaching or reiterating to him that God would supply what he needed to build the Temple and rule Israel.

This is an important key to renewing your mind. Many times God will reveal to you through revelation or inspiration what you need to do in your situation. You must be at peace within yourself so you can *hear* that still small voice,[72] so you can carry out God's will with a ready and willing mind.

In 1st Chronicles 28:21 David is reiterating the charge he gave Solomon in verse 9 [A]. Verse 20 should give Solomon peace of mind because David is encouraging him about how God will be with him in every way until the Temple is finished. Knowing that God would be working with him until the task was finished should bring great peace to your heart and allow him to *hear* any guidance from God's spirit in

---

[72] 1 Kings 19:11-12 KJV And he said, Go forth, and stand upon the mount before the LORD. And, behold, the LORD passed by, and a great and strong wind rent the mountains, and brake in pieces the rocks before the LORD; *but* the LORD *was* not in the wind: and after the wind an earthquake; *but* the LORD *was* not in the earthquake: 12 And after the earthquake a fire; *but* the LORD *was* not in the fire: and after the fire a still small voice.

him *(as verse 1st Chronicles 28:9 [A] states, as I expounded above).*

> **1 Chronicles 28:20 KJV**
> **20 And David said to Solomon his son, <u>Be strong</u> and of <u>good courage</u>, and do it: <u>fear not</u>, <u>nor be dismayed</u>: for the LORD God,** *even* **my <u>God, will be with thee;</u> <u>he will not fail thee, nor forsake thee,</u> <u>until thou hast finished all the work for the service of the house of the LORD.</u>**

Look at all these encouragements. This also should set our hearts at peace, so we can hear God's still small voice as we attend to His task. Why did I connect this verse to 1st Chronicles 28:9? Because I researched the structure of this chapter in Bullinger's Companion Bible[73] in which he has an extensive work on the structure in outline form. From Bullinger's research, Bullinger has 1st Chronicles 28:9-10, and 20-21 as complimenting charges from David to Solomon his son.

- Be Strong
- Be of good courage
- Fear not

---

[73] Bullinger, E.W. *(The Companion Bible)*, Zondervan Bible Publishers, Grand Rapids, Michigan. p. 566, Column 2, Ref Outline: *28.1-29. 8 PREPARATIONS. Outline ref: "r" (28:9-10, 28:20-21)*

- Don't be dismayed
- God will be with you until you have finished all the work for the service of the Temple (work) of the Lord.

See how all these are part of a peaceful soul, or peaceful understanding?

Now the [B]'s will be looked at.
[B] **Serve** *(Serve, labor for),*[74] with a **willing** *(desire, to take pleasure in),*[75] **mind** *(soul, life, the seat of your passions).*[76] Basically, you have a passion to labor for God, a desire to serve God. You want to willingly serve God with your life, it is your passion, your desire. See how these two [B]'s goes together? If we want to serve God, then we also need the right motivations, it is something we have a passion for, a desire for. We want to do it, so we can do God's will in our life. That is serving God.

In 1st Chronicles 28:21 we have more of David's encouragement to Solomon that reinforces 1st Chronicles 28:9 [B] as I just expounded above.

1 Chronicles 28:21 KJV

---

[74] Ibid., Meyers, Rich, Ref: H5647, def: 1-1a3
[75] Ibid., Meyers, Rich, Ref: H2655, def: 1
[76] Ibid., Meyers, Rich, Ref: H5315, def: 1

21 And, behold, the courses of the priests and the Levites, *even they shall be with thee* <u>**for all the service of the house of God:**</u> **and** *there shall be* **with thee for all manner of workmanship every** <u>**willing skilful man, for any manner of service:**</u> **also the princes and all the people** *will be* **wholly at thy commandment.**

You will notice the two phrases I underlined complement 1st Chronicles 28:9 [B], Serve God, with a willing heart, or life. The skilled workers were passionate to help build the Temple, and God worked with them as they worked in their trade in their service for God.

The second scripture I listed in 2nd Corinthians at the start of this sub-chapter is an example in the context where believers started out a year earlier with the right heart and motivation to collect some financial aid for Paul and the other Apostles, but only got as far as verbal or written commitments without collecting or sending the aid to the Apostles.

2 Corinthians 8:10-12 KJV
10 And herein I give *my* **advice: for this is expedient for you, who have begun before, not only to do, but also to be forward a year ago.**

11 Now therefore perform^(G2005) the doing *of it*; that as *there was* a readiness^(G4288) to will, so *there may be* a performance^(G2005) also out of that which ye have.
12 For if there be first a willing mind^(G4288), *it is* accepted according to that a man hath, *and* not according to that he hath not.

Here we have two repetitions of two separate Greek words. There is an overlap between them, and both have one of the Greek words outside the overlapping section. Each repetition has one of the other words that are repeated in an over-lap arrangement. The Greek words translated to English are accurate translations. I have given you the Greek in case you want to study these further.

- **perform, performance** *(G2005: epiteleō̄)*
- **readiness, a willing mind** *(G4288: prothumia)*

With repetitions like these in one or two verses, not only is the repeated word emphasized, the matter between the repeated words is also emphasized. And since each repeated set has one word from the other repeated set in between each repetition, both words used in both repetitions are emphasized.[77] As shown below in Italics and Bold fonts.

1) V11: *Perform (G2005)*

   a) V11: A readiness (G4288)

2) V11: *Performance (G2005)*

3) V12: A willing mind (G4288)

1) V11: Perform (G2005)

2) V11: *A readiness (G4288)*

   a) V11: Performance (G2005)

3) V12: *A willing mind (G4288)*

What is being emphasized?
BOTH! Having a WILLING MIND and having the PERFORMANCE of the thing they committed to do a year earlier. This repetition gives you the main topic in this section of 2nd Corinthians where Paul was reproving them for not carrying through on delivering the financial promise they made.

To truly renew your mind, you must not only make a promise to yourself to change something, you must also take some kind of *action* to carry out what you want to change or do. Just as Paul told the

---

[77] Bullinger, E.W. *(Figures of Speech used in the Bible)*, Baker Book House, Grand Rapids, Michigan.16th printing 1991. p. 261, **"Mesodiplosis" or, "Middle Repetition."** *The repetition of the same word or words in the middle of successive sentences* (or clauses).

Corinthians that *they (not God)* were responsible to carry out their promise to Paul in the collecting and delivering of the financial gift from the local believers. We also must take on the responsibility of acting on what we want to change or do. God will not take away or change your mind for you. You must do it by changing what you think and how you act in a new way to cause a change.

You must have a 1) Ready and Willing mind, and 2) You must perform the actions yourself.

This is the renewed mind. Paul was reinforcing the truth that it was up to each person to act on the promise that they made a year ago and finish the action needed to complete the task. Paul did not ask them to "pray to God" to help them finish what they started a year ago. Paul told them to finish what they started a year ago with a firm tone and held nothing back. It was up to the believers to correct their error in judgement and follow Paul's instructions and guidance.

The believers needed to <u>renew their willingness</u>, that is what Paul was addressing so they could receive the blessing God had for them.

7: The renewed mind: We choose who to believe

Romans 12:2 KJV
2 And be not conformed to this world: but be ye transformed by the renewing (G342) **of your mind, that ye may prove what** *is* **that good, and acceptable, and perfect, will of God.**

Titus 3:5 KJV
5 Not by works of righteousness which we have done, but according to his mercy he saved us, by the washing of regeneration, and renewing(G342) **of the Holy Ghost;**

These are the only two verses that contain the Greek noun **"anakainōsis"** *(G342)* which is translated **"renewing"** in the New Testament. The noun is from the Greek verb **"anakainoō"** *(G341)* which is translated **"renewed."** We will also look at the two verses that this word is used in. What is interesting is that both Greek words are used in two categories we are to work on "renewing," so we can be a Christian with knowledge and power!

Even though there are only four verses that contain two forms of the roots, *(G303: ana = up, G2537: kainos*

= *new*) that basically means to "new up" or "renovate" from a worse state to a better or new state. Here are the two verses that contain the verb form:

> **2 Corinthians 4:16 KJV**
> **16 For which cause we faint not; but though our outward man perish, yet the inward** *man* **is renewed**(G341) **day by day.**
>
> **Colossians 3:10 KJV**
> **10 And have put on the new** *man,* **which is renewed**(G341) **in knowledge** (G1922) *(precise and correct knowledge)* **after the image of him that created him:** *(renewed in a precise knowledge according to the spiritual creation in you)*

I have looked at a few words from the Greek in my more literal translation at the end of this verse. I have marked the word "knowledge" and inserted a basic meaning to help show this knowledge is more intense that than the word normally used for knowledge in the New Testament.

The Greek word normally used is the word **"gnōsis"** *(G1108)* which indicates a more general knowledge. The word used in Colossians 3:10 is the Greek word **"epignōsis"** which adds the prefix "epi" *(G1909)* to **"gnōsis."** **"EPI"** means: *on, or upon, generally, (on or* *upon knowledge)*. But **"epignōsis"** *(G1922)* when used metaphorically, adds a closer relationship than **"gnōsis"** *(G1108)*, therefore indicating a more precise knowledge of a thing studied and learned, compared to a less precise more general knowledge of **"gnōsis."**[78]

> *Summary of Colossians 3:10-11: We are to put on the new man, the Christ in us, and renovate our thoughts from a bad state to a better state with a precise knowledge of what God has given us in our new man, Christ in us, our gift holy spirit (what God created in us, that is; our spirit that He gave us). There is no Greek or Jew, circumcision nor uncircumcision, Barbarian, Scythian, bond or free, but Christ is in all, in the one body.*

Now, there is one more derivative of the verb form that is used in a totally different context, and in its context, it is stating that it is impossible to be born-again a second time, if a person has fallen away.

> **Hebrews 6:6 KJV**
> **6 If they shall fall away, to renew**[(G340)] **them again unto repentance; seeing they crucify to themselves the Son of**

---

[78] Meyers, Rick, (*Thayer's Greek Lexicon Dictionary*) E-Sword Software Version 11.1.0, Copyright ©2000-2017. Ref: 1909 **"epi;"** G1922 **"epignōsis,"** 1 and 1a.

Zodhiates, Spiros, Th.D., *(The Complete Word Study Dictionary: New Testament)*, AMG Publishers, Chattanooga, TN., Revised 1993. p. 624, Ref: 1922 **"epignōsis"** general definition.

God afresh, and put *him* to an open shame.

The context is not about losing your gift holy of spirit, it is about losing your fellowship. The Jewish-Christian believers had wrong thinking on the topic of "sonship" and confused it with the topic of "fellowship." It is a good example of how the Jewish-Christian believers had to *renew or change* their thinking to reflect what God's Word said, and then believe and act accordingly.

If you read and work Hebrews 6:4-6 it is obvious this is the subject. Work the words:

Heb 6:4 "impossible," "enlightened," "tasted," "heavenly gift," "partakers."
Heb 6:5 "tasted," "powers."
Heb 6:6 "shall fall away," "to renew," "again," "repentance."

Basically, it says from the Greek.... It is not possible since you partook of the heavenly gift (holy spirit) with its powers (9 manifestations), if you turn away from God (in your lifestyle, your mind) to renew, or get born-again, again with the gift holy spirit.

We need to look at the Greek words translated "renewing," and "renewed," and at several of the connected words as well.

The Greek word translated "renewing" in Romans 12:2 is "anakainōsis" (G342) and pronounced "an-ak-ah'ee-no-sis" and it is the noun form. It means: *(From G341, to make new), to renew qualitatively. Therefore, a renewing or a renovation which makes a person different than in the past.*[79] Thayer's: *a renewal, renovation, complete change for the better.*[80]

So, this word means generally, to renovate something for the better. Think about it, when you renovate something, you are replacing old worn out parts with either remanufactured parts or new parts. You are changing the older parts with newer parts to bring back the "like new" look and use of the product. Sometimes the older parts can be refurbished if they are not in too bad a condition, sometimes you need to totally replace the older part with a new part. Romans 12:2 gives us a specific category we need to renovate to be like new again.

> **Romans 12:1-2 KJV**
> **1 I beseech you therefore, brethren, by the mercies of God, that ye present your bodies a living sacrifice, holy,**

---

[79] Zodhiates, Spiros, Th.D., *(The Complete Word Study Dictionary: New Testament),* AMG Publishers, Chattanooga, TN., Revised 1993. p. 151, ref: 342, (341).

[80] Thayer, Joseph H., *(Thayer's Greek-English Lexicon of the New Testament),* Baker Books House, Grand Michigan, 24th printing. p. 38, ref: 342

acceptable unto God, *which* is your reasonable service.

2 And be not conformed to this world: but be ye transformed by the renewing(G342) **of your mind, that ye may prove what *is* that good, and acceptable, and perfect, will of God.**

We are to renovate our mind, or thoughts. But let's look at Romans 12:1 to see why we need to do this. We are to present ourselves a living sacrifice, holy and acceptable unto God, which is our reasonable or logical service unto God. How do we become a "living sacrifice" for God? Read the next verse. God wants us to prove His word, that His word is good, acceptable and perfect. There are over 900 promises for you to claim, you can only claim them by renewing your lifestyle, and that starts with your thoughts.

You can neither prove God's Word by living a materially poor life and sacrificing the good life God has for us, nor by becoming a "martyr for Jesus." God wants us to live a more than abundant lifestyle[81] by putting His word in our minds, by renovating our thoughts to think God's Word, and act on His word.

---

[81] John 10:10 KJV
10 The thief cometh not, but for to steal, and to kill, and to destroy: I am come that they might have life, and that they might have it more abundantly.

There are a few steps involved in Romans 12:2 that will help break down how we change our thoughts to line-up with God's Word, or thoughts.

1. **Be not conformed to this world**
2. **Be transformed by renovating your thoughts**
    a. So, you can prove that God's Word is
        i. Good
        ii. Acceptable
        iii. Perfect

The above general steps are your logical service to God because He has given you not only the gift of holy spirit now, but eternal life with the promise of the same type of spiritual body Jesus Christ has from His resurrection unto this day! And why do we want to renew our thoughts as outlined above? To serve the *one body*, to give back what God has given us. The next five verses bear this out being the immediate context of this section.

Our living sacrifice in the end is to serve the one body with what God has given us within the gift holy spirit, and any gift ministries God has bestowed upon us.

> Romans 12:3-8 KJV
> 3 For I say, through the grace given unto me, to every man that is among you, not to think *of himself* more highly than he

ought to think; but to think soberly, according as God hath dealt to every man the measure of faith.

4 For as we have many members in one body, and all members have not the same office:

5 So we, *being* many, are one body in Christ, and every one members one of another.

6 Having then gifts differing according to the grace that is given to us, whether prophecy, *let us prophesy* according to the proportion of faith;

7 Or ministry, *let us wait* on *our* ministering: or he that teacheth, on teaching;

8 Or he that exhorteth, on exhortation: he that giveth, *let him do it* with simplicity; he that ruleth, with diligence; he that sheweth mercy, with cheerfulness.

Now let's look at some of these steps and the connected words so we gain a fuller understanding of this process. The first step is to make a choice to not to fashion your beliefs or habit patterns how everyone else in the world forms theirs. God has always given us a choice on what our standard is to act on and live by, His Word, or the ways of this world.

7a: BE NOT CONFORMED (G4964-V) TO THIS WORLD

The word "conformed" in Romans 12:2 is the Greek verb "suschēmatizō" (G4964) and is pronounced "soos-khay-mat-id'-zo" which means: *To fashion, to fashion alike, conform to the same pattern outwardly.... In Romans 12:2, and expanded rendering might read: "Stop being molded by the external and fleeting fashions of this age, but undergo a deep inner change by the quantitative renewing of your mind."*[82]

The word is made up of two words, or the root word with a prefix.

The prefix is the Greek word: "sun" (G4862) and is pronounced "soon" and means: *A primary preposition denoting union; with or together* [83]

The root word in the Greek is the word: "schēma" (G4976) and is pronounced "skhay'-mah" and means: *From the alternate of G2192; a figure (as a mode*

---

[82] Zodhiates, Spiros, Th.D., (*The Complete Word Study Dictionary: New Testament*), AMG Publishers, Chattanooga, TN., Revised 1993. p. 1350, Ref: 4964

[83] Meyers, Rick, (*Strong's Hebrew and Greek Dictionary*) E-Sword Software Version 11.1.0, Copyright ©2000-2017. Ref: G4862

or circumstance), that is, (by implication) <u>*external condition*</u>*: - fashion.*[84]

We get the word "scheme" from this Greek word. The root word with the prefix refers to **"being united to the schemes of this world"** and they are controlled by the "god of this world *(age)*,"[85] Satan, in the bottom line.

These two words together can be translated *"a union with an external scheme."* That is, you are being united by your thoughts to be in line with something that you are allowing to change how you act and think from an outside force. You are being molded to accept certain habits and attitudes, certain schemes of this world. Satan's schemes result in "stealing, killing, and destroying" your dreams and goals in life.

> **John 10:10 KJV**
> **10 The thief cometh not, but for to steal, and to kill, and to destroy:** I am come that they might have life, and that they might have *it* more abundantly.

---

[84] Meyers, Rick, (*Strong's Hebrew and Greek Dictionary*) E-Sword Software Version 11.1.0, Copyright ©2000-2017. Ref: G4976

[85] 2 Corinthians 4:4 KJV
4 In whom the god of this world hath blinded the minds of them which believe not, lest the light of the glorious gospel of Christ, who is the image of God, should shine unto them.

We are not to be fashioned or molded by this world, *by outside influences*. What does that mean? It means we should not allow ourselves to be influenced by others around us, by their greediness or selfishness just because it can benefit us in the short and long run. It is about attitudes that influence us to change our habits from good to evil intent. There is a spiritual battle going on right now, even though Jesus Christ defeated Satan when he was raised from the dead. In our age, or grace administration, it is like the parable where the weeds and crop grow together, but at the harvest, at the return of Christ, they will be separated.

In the meantime, Satan has rule over the world and tries to mold you *with outside influences* to act through his ways, which will are selfish, prideful, and greedy, even in small "acceptable" ways that may seem to be acceptable to others, and you may think that there is no harm to others. This could happen in very subtle ways to push the boundaries of friendships or business dealings for personal gain and status to eventually live with attitudes and corresponding lifestyles that are conflicting with God's Word. This can happen over a long period of time so you don't notice the subtle change in your lifestyle until someone else you hold a lot of respect for, can no longer be your friend because of your change in attitude from good to evil intents.

Here are some verses that describe how we live in this world, and who governs this world while we wait for the return of Christ in the future w/o God's Word as our base.

> **1 Peter 1:14 KJV**
> **14 As obedient children, not fashioning yourselves**(G4964-V) **according to the former lusts in your ignorance:**
>
> **Ephesians 2:2-3 KJV**
> **2 <u>Wherein in time past ye walked according to the course of this world, according to the prince of the power of the air,</u> the spirit that now worketh in the children of disobedience:**
> **3 Among whom also we all had our conversation in times past in the lusts of our flesh, fulfilling the desires of the flesh and of the mind; and were by nature the children of wrath, even as others.**

We are to put on God's Word and operate the manifestations of holy spirit if we are going to truly renew our minds and live God's Word and not allow our adversary to mold us in *his* ways, which would make God's Word null and void in our lives. The battle is in our mind, in what we think and act on, daily, every day. Therefore, we must stay diligent to learn and apply God's Word, and not be molded after the ways of this world *by outside influences*, so we can stand in this day, and benefit from God's promises now. This is how to defeat the schemes of the adversary, so we are not molded by his corrupt ways and attitudes. These are the ways to be **transformed**, not conformed, so we prove that God's Word is good and acceptable and perfect; to deny the adversary his influence in our life. I will get more into "transforming" in the next sub-chapter

> **Ephesians 6:11-13 KJV**
> **11 Put on the whole armour of God, that ye may be able to stand against the wiles** *(trickery or deceit)* **of the devil.**
> **12 For we wrestle not against flesh and blood, but against principalities, against powers, against the rulers of the darkness of this world, against spiritual wickedness in high** *places.*
> **13 Wherefore take unto you the whole armour of God, that ye may be able to withstand in the evil day, and having done all, to stand.**

We are to take on the whole armour of God, so we can stand against the deceitfulness of Satan who is trying to mold us into his agents against God. It is through *words* that we believe and act on, we must make sure we act on God's words, and not Satan's words, or schemes. Let's look at some verses that give us a choice to act on God's Word and receive His blessings, or act on *(be conformed to)* Satan's word and receive his cursing.

> **Ephesians 4:28 KJV**
> **28 Let him that stole steal no more: but rather let him labour, working with *his* hands the thing which is good, that he may have to give to him that needeth.**

What is one of the devil's schemes? Stealing from others by not working to meet your needs. How do you not be *conformed* to that scheme? You work a job that is honest work and it will meet your needs, and you give from your disposable or extra earnings or talent to those that have a need.

> **Ephesians 4:29 KJV**
> **29 Let no corrupt communication proceed out of your mouth, but that which is good to the use of edifying, that it may minister grace unto the hearers.**

What is another one of the devil's schemes? Having a conversation that is worthless for the hearer and may very well cause bad feelings in the other person, it does not edify them, but instead it tears them down. How do you not *conform* to that scheme? You speak edifying words which minister grace *(unmerited favour)* to them.

Here are some more attitudes and actions that are orchestrated by Satan to harm yourself and others in the long run. You may not see how it harms you or them right now, but, either in this life, or later, after the return of Christ, you will reap the consequences. After the return, as a born-again believer, you will lose any rewards that you would have gained if you chose to be corrupted in those situations.

The works of the flesh are what grows in a person's life as they keep living in the corruption of attitudes against God's Word. It is also fruit because of the context of this section. This section is describing two kinds of fruit, "fruit of the spirit *(Galatians 5:22-23)*, and the "works *(fruit)* of the flesh" *(Galatians 5:19-21)*. When you live under corrupt thoughts and habits, the fruit will also be corrupt. I will provide the list from these verses concerning the "works *(fruit)* of the flesh" with a better translation with the Greek word referenced. I will use one footnote to cite the Greek dictionary that I used.[86]

The reason the word "works" is used is because "works" can produce negative and positive

---

[86] Thayer, Joseph H., *(Thayer's Greek-English Lexicon of the New Testament)*, Baker Books House, Grand Michigan, 24th printing.

outcomes. But, the word "fruit" is only used about positive outcomes that come from operating the gift of holy spirit and renewing your mind to act on God's Word. Fruit can only produce positive results, not negative.

> Galatians 5:19-21 KJV
> 19 Now the works of the flesh are manifest, which are *these;* Adultery, fornication, uncleanness, lasciviousness,
> 20 Idolatry, witchcraft, hatred, variance, emulations, wrath, strife, seditions, heresies,
> 21 Envyings, murders, drunkenness, revellings, and such like: of the which I tell you before, as I have also told *you* in time past, that they which do such things shall not inherit the kingdom of God.

1. **Adultery,** G3430: only sexual
2. **fornication,** G4202: sexual and spiritual
3. **uncleanness,** G167: immoral motives and actions
4. **lasciviousness,** G766: unbridled lust, insolence
5. **Idolatry,** G1495: the worship of false gods

6. **witchcraft,** G5331: the use of drugs, poisoning, and sorcery for deceiving and seduction
7. **hatred,** G2189: hostility, adversarial, hateful
8. **variance,** G2054: contentious, strife
9. **emulations,** G2205: jealous, rivalry
10. **wrath,** G2372: quick to anger, easily angered
11. **strife,** G2052: causes division for self-promotion
12. **seditions,** G1370: causing dissention
13. **heresies,** G139: dissention by forming opposing groups, or opinions
14. **envyings,** G5355: jealousy
15. **murders,** G5408: to slay, kill, murder
16. **drunkenness,** G3178: intoxicated, this is an ongoing habit or obsession
17. **revellings,** G3970: rioters, in the sense of being partially drunk and going outside to stir up trouble, to be loud and annoying.

These are all "schemes" from Satan, the god of this world to cause you slip-up in living God's Word so you can't defeat his power and influence over your life. These are all actions that can form as habits in your life and become as second nature. These will all cause a believer to break their "fellowship," *(not "sonship")* with God, and they will not see God's promises come to pass in their life. To read more about how to get back in fellowship with God, read 1st John. The whole book is about our fellowship with God and it reveals plenty of God's logic on how we can have it. Pay attention to chapter one verses 6-10 for details on what you need to do so you can maintain that fellowship. Also re-read chapter four in this book for an expanded look at fellowship and how to stay in fellowship. Fellowship is part of our relationship with God through Christ Jesus; it allows us to be in harmony with our spirit and mind. That is why there are two areas we need to build up, our spirit and our mind *(thoughts that turned into habits)*.

It's very interesting to note when you look at the context of this section in Galatians chapter 5 -- it is comparing two types of actions or attitudes that a person can choose from. There is the lifestyle based on the schemes from this world that results in the **"works of the flesh"** which is one choice; and the lifestyle based on living by God's Word including manifesting the gift of holy spirit that results in the **"fruit of the spirit,"** which is the other choice. God has always given us a choice. God has also described each choice and the results of choosing one or the other. In this chapter we are looking at a choice between living by the ways of the world which are selfish and greedy or to live by the words of God which are loving and giving. It is our choice and this chapter in Galatians lays it out quite clearly.

There are other chapters in the Epistles that also show us the schemes of the world like the list I provided above that can add to your understanding. They are all in direct opposition to the fruit of the spirit. That is one choice that we have, and many people take that choice because they see the immediate profit and that's all they're concerned about. That choice is the choice to be conformed to this world by the schemes of our adversary who wants to make sure that your habits and actions are in direct opposition to the true word of God.

The other choice we have is to be transformed by the renewing of our minds to form new habits and actions from the inside that are in direct alignment with God's Word so that we can produce the fruit of the spirit which is in direct opposition to the works of the flesh. You can't have both habits or actions in your life at the same time. You can either love at any one moment or you can hate at any one moment for example, but you can't love and hate at the same moment in time.

Therefore, Paul says in Galatians 5:16 and 17 that if you walk in the spirit you shall not fulfill the lust of the flesh.

> **Galatians 5:16-17 KJV**
> **16** *This* **I say then, Walk in the Spirit, and ye shall not fulfil the lust of the flesh.**
> **17 For the flesh lusteth against the Spirit, and the Spirit against the flesh: and these are contrary the one to the other: so that ye cannot do the things that ye would.**

That's what Paul is talking about, you can't live both attitudes and actions at the same time. Once you make a choice you either live by the action and attitude of the spirit or you live by the action and attitude of the lusts of the flesh which are in this context of the schemes of the world. In the next subchapter we will be looking at transforming our habits and actions to be in alignment with God's Word so that we can have the fruit of the spirit in our lives instead of the works of the flesh.

7b: BUT BE YE TRANSFORMED(G3339-V) BY THE RENEWING(G342-N) OF YOUR MIND(G3563-N)

To be transformed is to change from the inside; it is to totally change your thoughts to form new habits that replace the old habits that are no longer wanted. The Greek word behind the word "transformed" is where we get the English word "metamorphosis." When a caterpillar goes through this process to become a butterfly, the caterpillar is internally changed, and the new form is now a butterfly on the outside, it is a new creation, a new creature. The caterpillar literally no longer exists and emerges out of its cacoon as a totally new creature. We are a new creation "in-Christ." The phrase "in-Christ" implies within its context that we have renewed our thoughts to live in the truth of God's Word. That is, we are now transformed in the areas we have renewed our minds to be a new creation in-Christ.[87] But to have the completely new body like the butterfly has will have to be fulfilled at the return of Christ.

In the interim, we can renew our mind *(our thoughts that turn into habits)* and become a new creation within the limitations our physical mind's ability to live and walk by our spirit in us. This gift of holy spirit is a down payment, not all of the available power, but what we need now. And we will get our

---

[87] 2 Corinthians 5:17 KJV
17 Therefore if any man be in Christ, he is a new creature: old things are passed away; behold, all things are become new.

new body and mind, along with the rest our power when Christ returns.

> **Colossians 3:2 KJV**
> **2 Set your affection** *(thoughts)* **on things above** *(spiritual matters)*, **not **on things** on the earth** *(carnal things)*. *One possible literal considering the comparison:*
>
> *"Be devoted through your mindset on the heavenly, or spiritual matters – the things from God – and not the earthly things from the god of this world."*
>
> ** *"On things" is not a repetition in the text as translated in the KJV.*

This is the first thing we need to change: we need to think on what God's Word says and change our attitudes and actions to what we should have in order to receive His blessings. We need to change our devotions *(mindset)* from "the schemes of this world" to the "life principles" in God's Word. We need to stop living by the attitudes and actions from the "works of the flesh" and start living in "the fruit of the spirit."

Have you noticed that in order to **"stop"** one negative attitude and action you must **"start"** another positive attitude and action to replace it?

That is how you "set your thoughts" or "set your mindset" on the spiritual matters in God's Word. You replace one old thought with another new thought along with its corresponding actions.

You can pray for God to help you, but you can't pray for God to do it for you! *("God, please take away stealing from me, in Jesus name I pray." This kind of prayer goes against God's promise <u>not</u> to violate your freedom of will).*

You are the only one who controls your thoughts and actions. You are the only one who controls what you think and act on. You are the only one who must "stop" thinking and acting by the "works of the flesh," and you are the only one who[88] must "start" thinking and acting on what the Word of God teaches.

The phrase "Set your affections on" in Colossians 3:2 is the one Greek word: "phroneō" (G5426) and

---

[88] Bullinger, E.W. *(Figures of Speech used in the Bible)*, Baker Book House, Grand Rapids, Michigan.16th printing 1991. p. 199, **"Anaphora; or Like Sentence Beginnings."** Def: *The repetition of the same word* (by extension: phrase) *at the beginning of successive sentences.... This figure is so-called because it is the repeating of the same word* (by extension: phrase) *at the beginning of successive clauses: thus adding weight and emphasis to statements and arguments by calling special attention to them.* (It is okay for authors to incorporate figures of speech in their writings to bring out certain conditions or points for the reader. Don't let modern guidelines hinder you, as authors, we need to keep the use of figures of speech alive in our writings in the applicable places, or we will lose them).

is pronounced "fron-eh'-o" and means: - *To think, have a mindset, be minded. **The activity represented by this word involves the will, affections, and conscience.**"* - For Col. 3:2: IIBa: *To be mindful of, to be devoted to (Matt. 16:23; Mk. 8:33; Rom. 8:5; Phil. 3:19; Col. 3:2).*[89]

In order to change your thoughts and actions, you must have the **"will,"** the **"affections or concerns,"** and the **"conscience or morality"** to start to honestly change from a worse state of mind to a better state of mind by the transformation of renewing your mind *(or thoughts)*. When you have a "mindset" you are locked in your understanding and determined to think and act in a certain way. This is what it takes to truly change your mind from one set of thoughts and actions to another, a more productive set of thoughts and actions that will be the new mindset for your lifestyle in any area you are working on.

That is what the renewed mind goal is, to change your old worldly scheme lifestyle that is corrupt in nature to serve your selfish desires, and to be transformed by a new godly lifestyle that is not selfish or corrupt in nature, so God can bless you in all your endeavours.

---

[89] Zodhiates, Spiros, Th.D., *(The Complete Word Study Dictionary: New Testament),* AMG Publishers, Chattanooga, TN., Revised 1993. p. 1454, Ref: 5426 General definition + IIBa

Romans 12:2 KJV
2 And be not conformed to this world: but be ye transformed by the renewing of your mind, that ye may prove what is that good, and acceptable, and perfect, will of God.

In this sub-chapter we will be looking how we transform our mind *(thoughts)* by renewing *(renovating)* our thoughts to think and act on what the Word of God teaches us about living His Word in a practical way.

The three words we will look at are: **"transformed," "renewed,"** and **"mind."**

- The word **"transformed" is what** we want to do,
- The word **"renewing" is how** we do it, and
- The word **"mind" is where** we do it.

There are also "connected" words related to this study that give us more detail on **how** to accomplish our goal to be transformed. Three such phrases we will look at are: **"put on," "put off,** and **"in Christ."** But first, we must look at our initial three words that are shaded in Romans 12:2 above.

The first word we will look at is the word translated **"transformed"** which is in direct contrast to being

"conformed." Conformed is pressure from an outside source that keeps the pressure on until you are molded to the point where you will maintain the shape of the mold after the pressure is released. Picture a coin operated toy mold machine at the zoo that can make a plastic molded Elephant from molten plastic. You insert your money and the two halves of the mold come together to provide the shape of the toy. The molten plastic is released in the mold and pressure is used on the molten plastic to force it to dry in the shape of the mold. When the molten plastic is hard enough to keep the shape of the mold, the finished toy is released from the mold, and is dropped into the finished drawer for the customer to take out.

The word "transform" has to do with changing the form also, it is used of our thoughts, and our outside appearance at the return of Christ. The transformation in Romans 12:2 is happening from inside our brain right now, through our thoughts. This word is used in both kinds of transformation in the Bible, referring to our new spiritual body and our thoughts from our brain.

The word "transformed" in Romans 12:2 is the Greek word: "metamorphoō" (G3339) and is pronounced "met-am-or-fo'-o" and means: *from - metá- G3326 denoting change of place or condition and* *from -morphoō- G3445 to form. To transform, transfigure, change one's form.*[90]

The referenced dictionary only mentions a physical transformation, but in the few uses in the New Testament, there are two categories, not one category, therefore we must separate them to rightly divide this word in its context. In two out of the four uses, it is used in the context of Jesus Christ being "transfigured" into his future new spiritual body before some of the Apostles. In one it is used in the context of transforming our thoughts. In one it is used as we look at ourselves in a mirror as Moses might have looked with God's glory shown about him. *(I put this in the category of the "renewed mind" of Moses)* This last one may be how God and Christ Jesus along with the angels see us now as we are living the renewed mind.

Categories: Transformed
1. **Our new bodies** in the future when Christ returns. Matt 17:2, Mark 9:2
2. **Our new thoughts**, while we wait for the return, and how we are seen by God's spiritual realm. Romans 12:2, 2nd Corinthians 13:8

---

[90] Zodhiates, Spiros, Th.D., *(The Complete Word Study Dictionary: New Testament)*, AMG Publishers, Chattanooga, TN., Revised 1993. p. 968, Ref: 3339, General definition of the two words it is made from, noted above.

Because there are not that many uses of the combined Greek word with the prefix **metá**, we will also look at the root word and related words for more uses to gain a better understanding. There are only a half dozen or so, and we need to put on our thinker for some verses. First, the full Greek word is used in category two. In Romans 12:2 we have the third use and the context changes the topic from seeing a changed future spiritual body to changing our mind. Just as at the return we will also be changed or receive our new spiritual body, our mind can also be changed to take on a whole new pattern of thoughts that are godly, not earthly. And our new way of life through our new thinking patterns will shine in this world as Moses' countenance shined for the Israelites after he came down after speaking with God. Spiritually that is how we shine in this world to the spirit realm when we are living by the renewed mind now.

> **Romans 12:2 KJV**
> **2 And be not conformed to this world: but be ye transformed by the renewing of your mind**, that ye may prove what is that good, and acceptable, and perfect, will of God.

If you read Romans 12:1ff, you'll notice that the context is talking about changing your thoughts from thoughts that are bad or corrupt to thoughts that are good or godly according to God's Word. Obviously, we are not to be transformed in our physical form, which is the other category. But we are to be transformed in our minds. So just as Jesus Christ was transfigured in front of some of his apostles, that is, his physical body changed form to look like a spiritual body, our thoughts will also change from corrupt to godly as we renew our thoughts. The Apostles and Jesus Christ got a glimpse of the future body God has for them. When we renew our mind or our thoughts, it is literally changing our old thought patterns to being new thought patterns. And the old thought patterns no longer exist except for our memory of them. Just as when we receive our new spiritual body our old physical body will no longer exist.

The word "metamorphosis" means: *1) a complete change of form, structure, or substance…<u>2) any complete change in appearance, character, circumstances etc</u>. 3) a form resulting from any change.*[91]

As you can see in the definition above, a change or transformation can take place with the person's character, which would be controlled by their thoughts. The reason I bring this up is because of the word "mind" in Romans 12:2, which is the object we

---

[91] Webster's., *(Webster's Encyclopedic Unabridged Dictionary of the English Language)*, Portland House 1997 a division of Random House Value Publishing, NY, New York. p. 900 column 3, **"metamorphosis"**

are to transform. We are to transform our minds, or thoughts by "renewing" it. The "renewing" is the action we take to transform our minds or thoughts. So, we have a "goal," an "action or how," and "what" we are to change.

The word "mind" in Romans 12:2 is the Greek noun: "nous" (G3563) and is pronounced "nooce" a which means: *General definition: Mind, the organ of mental perception and apprehension, of conscious life, of consciousness preceding actions or recognizing and judging them, intelligent understanding.* **By extension: (I)** *As the seat of emotions and affections, mode of thinking and feeling, disposition, moral inclination, equivalent to the heart. (Rom. 1:28; 12:2; 1st Cor. 1:10; Eph. 4:17, 23; Col. 2:18; 1st Tim. 6:5; 2nd Tim. 3:8; Titus 1:15).*[92]

As with most words in any language, the meaning is controlled by the context it is used in. It can have shades of meanings that deviate from the general meaning with a more nuanced definition that is more context specific. This word is no different, although the main meaning is talking about the mind as our physical brain, this word is also used as different functions of our brain. In Romans 12:2, it is used as

---

[92] Zodhiates, Spiros, Th.D., *(The Complete Word Study Dictionary: New Testament),* AMG Publishers, Chattanooga, TN., Revised 1993. p. 1017-1018, Ref: 3563, General def. plus (I)

the "seat of our personal lives," "our hearts, or inner most convictions.

This nuance involves our thought processes being settled on certain ideas and premises that we have used to form habits and actions to agree with them. This is one function of our brain or mind. This area is what we are to transform or change, we are to transform our heart, our inner most convictions that control our habits and actions. The only way to do that is to change what we think and how we respond in situations. We need to change our inner convictions that are contrary to God's Word, so they align themselves with God's Word.

Paul gave some rather detailed information on this process in Romans 7:1ff that helps us understand the frustration we will have when we are trying to transform our corrupt habits and actions to godly habits and actions. Paul went through this frustration also, and God had him share his understanding and how he overcame it with God's Word.

> **Romans 7:25 KJV**
> **25 I thank God through Jesus Christ our Lord. So then with the mind I myself serve the law** *(word)* **of God; but with the flesh the law of sin** *(flesh)*.

This verse is Paul's conclusion about his frustration with the old thoughts he is replacing with the new thoughts.

The old thoughts are trying to overcome the new thoughts before they become established.

Paul goes through the process that he is battling in his mind, so he can have the strength to keep the old thoughts null and void. Paul shares that until the return of Christ we will have this battle in our mind. He separates the "carnal man" from the "spiritual man" by letting us know that the "carnal man" is dead "in Christ" *(indicating when we act with the renewed mind – in Christ – our bad habits are dead to us)* and even though he is living in the renewed mind, corrupt thoughts still plague his mind at times, he has to reject them and keep and do God's Word. You can see how aggravating this can get. Let's read this section, I will insert notes on a verse right after the verse if needed.

Paul's reasoning starts from before there was a written or word for mankind to follow. Therefore, mankind could not know what sin was. *(This is an illustration to allow us to better understand what he is sharing).* The logic is simple, if I had no rules to live by, then there are no rules, and everything I do is okay to do because there are no restrictions. I can conclude then that sin does not exist. It was only after the rules came that I found out that I was committing offences against the regulations.

It was then I found out what I thought was life without regulations, turned out to be sin or death after I knew the regulations. I then found out after knowing the regulations and trying to live by them, that my old ways before the regulations did not want to stop being active either. So, I had a battle in my mind between the old ways and the new ways that were always fighting for dominance in my life. I had to choose which "way" to act on, and which "way" to pay no attention to. I concluded that I can serve God by living His Word through my renewed mind, by living by God's rules, but with the flesh *(when I mess up and give in to the old ways)* I will serve sin. Paul realized he was not perfect in the flesh, and he would mess up at times *(and he did)*. But he also realized that he was perfect "in Christ" when he acted with his renewed mind.

> **Romans 7:7-25 KJV**
> **7 What shall we say then? Is the law sin? God forbid. Nay, I had not known sin, but by the law: for I had not known lust, except the law had said, Thou shalt not covet.**
> **8 But sin, taking occasion by the commandment, wrought in me all**

manner of concupiscence. For without the law sin was dead.

9 For I was alive without the law once: but when the commandment came, sin revived, and I died.

10 And the commandment, which was ordained to life, I found to be unto death.

11 For sin, taking occasion by the commandment, deceived me, and by it slew me.

12 Wherefore the law is holy, and the commandment holy, and just, and good.

13 Was then that which is good made death unto me? God forbid. But sin, that it might appear sin, working death in me by that which is good; that sin by the commandment might become exceeding sinful.

14 For we know that the law is spiritual: but I am carnal, sold under sin. *(Adam sold mankind's power and dominion to Satan when he disobeyed God's only restriction)*

15 For that which I do I allow not: for what I would, that do I not; but what I hate, that do I. *(The things he doesn't want to do... he does)*

16 If then I do that which I would not, I consent unto the law that it is good *(fair,*

honest). (If I do the things I don't what to do, I join with the regulations that they are fair)
17 Now then <u>it is no more I that do it, but sin that dwelleth in me.</u> *(It is not me through the renewed mind that does it, but sin or disobedience that still dwells in me)*
18 For I know that in me (that is, in my flesh,) dwelleth no good thing: for to will is present with me; but how to perform that which is good I find not. *(I know in areas where I have not renewed my mind is disobedience, my flesh. But my will to do God's Word is with me, but how to act on it, I find not… in my flesh). The word "flesh" stands for us when we are living by the schemes of the world, not by the renewed mind.*
19 For the good that I would I do not: but the evil which I would not, that I do. *(the result of verse 18, he walks by the flesh)*
20 Now if I do that I would not, <u>it is no more I that do it, but sin that dwelleth in me.</u> *(This is repeated from verse 17)*
21 I find then a law, that, when I would do good, evil is present with me. *(As long as we are alive before the return of Christ, we will have both kind of thoughts in our minds, we will always have a choice to make).*
22 For I delight in the law of God after the inward man:

23 But I see another law in my members, warring against the law of my mind, and bringing me into captivity to the law of sin which is in my members. *(It is a battle of thoughts - God's Word or the thoughts generated from the schemes of this world.)*
24 O wretched man that I am! who shall deliver me from the body of this death? *(At the return of Christ, we receive a new mind, new knowledge where only righteous thoughts can dwell)*
25 I thank God through Jesus Christ our Lord. So then with the mind I myself serve the law of God; but with the flesh the law of sin. *(We serve God via the renewed mind in areas that have been transformed by God's Word)*

Here are some more verses with the Greek word "nous" meaning: the seat of the emotions, disposition, moral inclination, that is, your inner most heart.

Romans 1:28 KJV
28 And even as they did not like to retain God in *their* **knowledge, God gave them over to a reprobate mind, to do those things which are not convenient;**

This is used in a negative context where men and women refused to hold on to God's Word by their acknowledgement of God. So, God surrendered them over to a reprobate *(worthless)* heart. God's mercy and grace can only go so far, but when a person has refused God's mercy and grace so many times, God allows them to reap their consequences according to their heart. God gave the Pharaoh of Egypt many chances to change his heart toward Moses and the Israelites. After the plagues were over, the Pharaoh still refused to change and let Moses and the Israelites go, by this time it was obvious that the Pharaoh was not going to heed God's warnings from Moses. God had no choice at that point but to allow the Pharaoh to reap the consequences of his actions. The Same thing is happening here in Romans 1:28.

Another negative use is in Ephesians chapter 4 that talks about a similar mind set as Romans 1:28. I have included some of the verses to show the context.

> **Ephesians 4:17-19 KJV**
> **17 This I say therefore, and testify in the Lord, that ye henceforth walk not as other Gentiles walk, in the vanity of their mind,**
> **18 Having the understanding darkened, being alienated from the life of God**

through the ignorance that is in them, because of the blindness of their heart: **19 Who being past feeling <u>have given themselves over</u> unto lasciviousness, to work all uncleanness with greediness.**

Ephesians has a similar phrase to the phrase "gave them over" in Romans 1:28 which is the same Greek word used in Ephesians 4:19 translated as "have given *themselves* over." But with the added word that indicates that it was because of **their** continual unrighteous actions in their lifestyle. This gives further details about what caused the unrighteousness in Romans 1:28 and the immediate context. God calls this type of behaviour "...walk *(live)* not as other Gentiles walk *(live)*, in the vanity *(depravity or immortality)* of their mind *(heart)*. If you read verses 18-19, you will read about some of this "immorality" the Gentiles lived by in their heart.

1 Corinthians 1:10 KJV
10 Now I beseech you, brethren, by the name of our Lord Jesus Christ, that ye all ¹<u>speak the *same thing*</u>, and *that* **there be ²<u>no divisions among you</u>; but** *that* **ye be ³<u>perfectly joined together</u> in the ⁴<u>*same* mind</u> and in the ⁵<u>*same* judgment</u>.**

In this context we read how Paul was reproving them for being divided about God's Word and encouraged them to have the same moral inclination, the same disposition, the same heart. But, to get there, they also had to work on five things in their renewed mind with corresponding actions.

➡1. **"Speak the same thing."** That is, to affirm the same thing, in the context, to affirm the same rightly divided word of God, the same values.
   2. **"No divisions among** *(with or in)* **you."** They were to have no more divisions or schisms in interpreting God's Word. When everyone speaks the same rightly divided Word, there will be no divisions on what God's Word says.
   3. **"Perfectly joined together."** That is, their divisions needed to be repaired perfectly, that is, no schisms in their understanding of God's Word. So, they could resolve any divisions on what God's Word meant because they would now agree on God's rightly divided word, without any divisions by private interpretation.
➡4. **"The same mind** *(heart)*.**"** They were to be perfectly joined together with the same convictions or mindset on what the Word said.
➡5. **"The same judgement."** And they were to be perfectly joined together in the same advice, values, or counsel from the rightly divided Word.

If you have noticed, in order to **"speak the same thing"** (#1), numbers 2-5 need to be carried out. And there is also a **"repetition"** in this verse that puts the extra emphasis on three of the five things listed. These three things that contain the repetition of the word **"same"** are the main areas of importance.

1. **"Speak the same thing"** to affirm the same Word of God's meaning by rightly dividing His Word.
2. Being perfectly joined together in **"the same mind"** *(mindset, heart)*.
3. Being perfectly joined together in **"the same judgement"** or the same counsel or advice from God's Word. This would be from the values that God's Word teaches like moral values for instance.

Just look at how one verse has so much to offer us in teaching us how to live within the one body of Christ so that our local family of God can grow and thrive!

In Ephesians 4:21-32 we read how to make a choice and change the unrighteous areas in our lives by renewing our "heart," our inner most being, to live God's Word, and not live by our former behaviour. That is, how to get rid of any divisions in how to live God's Word, which is one of the main topics in this section in Ephesians 4:17ff. Look at Ephesians 4:23, which is a very concise and powerful verse in instructing us on the renewed mind.

> **Ephesians 4:23 KJV**
> **23 And be renewed** *(renovated)* **in the spirit** *(life)* **of your mind;** *(inner most heart).*

We are instructed to renovate *(or make like new)* the life of our inner most heart, where we live by first nature habits that are so much a part of ourselves, that we automatically act out without any thought. It is in those bad habits *(that are corrupt in nature because they are against God and His Word)* that we are to renew *(renovate like new)* that will give us a new life to our inner most heart. The phrase "and be renewed" is an encouragement for us to make a choice between our former behaviour and a new behaviour to live by God's Word. God has always given us a choice.

The word "renewed" in Ephesians 4:23 is the Greek word "ananeóō" (G365) and is pronounced "an-an-neh-o'-o" and means: *To renew, make young.*[93]

The word "spirit" in Ephesians 4:23 is the Greek word "pneuma" (G4151) and is pronounced

---

[93] Zodhiates, Spiros, Th.D., *(The Complete Word Study Dictionary: New Testament),* AMG Publishers, Chattanooga, TN., Revised 1993. p. 155, Ref 365.

"pnyoo'-mah" and it means: *in a figurative way* "*meaning the individual entity or self. Such as myself, yourself, himself, the seat of operation of man's personal life, often referred to as "heart." (a) The issues that result from the operation of a man's mind such as acts of will, thoughts, desires, emotions.*[94]

The word "mind" in Ephesians 4:23 is the Greek word "nous" (G3563)[95]

> Colossians 2:18 KJV
> 18 <u>Let no man beguile you of your reward in a voluntary humility and worshipping of angels, intruding into those things which he hath not seen, vainly puffed up by his fleshly mind</u>,

This verse gives us guidance and knowledge on one of the ways our adversary will try to steal our renewed minds *(including future rewards)* from us. Did you know that we will receive rewards after the return of Christ for renewing our mind to any and all areas we change in to live God's Word? But these rewards can be stolen from us if we allow the schemes of this world to overcome us in the areas

---

[94] Wierwille, V.P., *(Receiving the holy spirit today)*, American Christian Press, New Knoxville, Ohio 1982. p. 239 Appendix III, p. 286 Appendix II.
[95] Zodhiates, Spiros, Th.D., *(The Complete Word Study Dictionary: New Testament)*, AMG Publishers, Chattanooga, TN., Revised 1993. p. 1017-1018, Ref: 3563, General def. plus (I) *(see page 213 above for the full definition)*

that we have worked so hard on. Our adversary wants to replace our new, godly habits with our old unrighteous habits, causing an un-renewed mind and a loss of rewards.

I have underlined some words in this verse that we will need to look at and understand in a better translation or meaning. This verse is essential to understand because it uses an Old English term and some of the translated words could have been more accurate in English. This is the case in many verses where the translators want to hide, mislead, or make the verse harder to understand by using obsolete or rarely used phrases and steer the reader towards their church dogma, and away from the truth from God's Word.

The first phrase "let no man" is one Greek word (G3367) and is translated somewhat correctly. It could translate to "Don't let no one *(anyone)* **whoever he may be."**[96]

The next phrase "beguile ~~you~~ **of your reward" is two Greek words, the word "you" (G5209) is a separate word in the Greek. "Beguile of your reward" is the Greek word (G2603). A better translation could be "defraud or deprive you of the**

---

[96] Zodhiates, Spiros, Th.D., *(The Complete Word Study Dictionary: New Testament)*, AMG Publishers, Chattanooga, TN., Revised 1993. p. 980, Ref: 3367, general definition.

prize or reward *[from your Christian observance of God's Word]."*[97]

The next phrase **"in a voluntary humility and worshipping of angels"** is a little difficult to understand due to the Old English terminology. It could be better translated to **"Out of pretended humility, they worshipped** *[misleading]* **angels."**[98]

The next phrase "<u>intruding into those things which he hath not seen</u>" is a good translation referring to the worshipping of misleading angels of which they have no knowledge. They think they are the true God's angles that are guiding them. The next phrase tells us they are fooled.

I must slow down and explain what is happening, and what has happened in the past that caused the true believers to follow doctrines that sounded like the true doctrine. Over time, the leadership would add slight changes to the true doctrine that was accepted by the masses and eventually accepted as the original doctrine from God. But it was in fact false doctrine from the leadership that dismantled the true

---

[97] Ibid., Zodhiates, Spiros, Th.D., p. 827, Ref: 2603, general definition.

[98] Meyers, Rick, *(John Westley Commentary)*, E-Sword Software Version 11.1.0, Copyright ©2000-2017. "**Out of pretended humility, they worshipped angels,** as not daring to apply immediately to God. Yet this really sprung from their being puffed up: (the constant forerunner of a fall, Pro 16:18) so far was it from being an instance of true humility."

Word of God but sounding very religious to the masses.

This was done over an extended period, and the masses thought they were doing God's Will and earning rewards for the future when Christ returns. But they were not earning any rewards at all because they were not doing God's will. The leaders were being influenced by pride, greed, and power over their congregation. This was done spiritually from the god of this world, Satan who infiltrated the leadership through the promise of power and greed that would make them wealthy and powerful in their community, and possibly worldwide. The leadership was blind to the methods of their adversary and did not realize they were being manipulated to cause their congregation to abandon the true Word of God for their doctrines of men that sounded religious and true.

This happened to most of the leaders in the Old Testament, and it was happening to some leaders in the New Testament also. Paul warned of this in 1st Timothy chapter 1 and had other advice for leadership. In Titus Paul recommended vetting new leadership to have minimum leadership standards. In 2nd Timothy Paul encouraged the leadership in several areas to stand strong and keep preaching the Word of God. Timothy is addressed to the church leadership. So, it was the leadership that was getting fooled, and then teaching error to the masses. Their "commandments of men" were replacing and making null and void God's Word in their life.

The believers "looked and acted" religious, but they had no spiritual power in their lives anymore. Their gift of holy spirit was, in essence shut down.

> 1 Timothy 4:1 KJV
> 1 Now the Spirit speaketh expressly, that in the latter times some shall depart from the faith, giving heed to seducing spirits, and doctrines of devils;
>
> Matthew 15:7-9 KJV
> 7 Ye hypocrites, well did Esaias prophesy of you, saying,
> 8 This people draweth nigh unto me with their mouth, and honoureth me with their lips; but their heart is far from me.
> 9 But in vain they do worship me, teaching for doctrines the commandments of men.
>
> Matthew 15:3 KJV
> 3 But he answered and said unto them, Why do ye also transgress the commandment of God by your tradition (commandments of men)?

The last phrase in Colossians 2:18 "vainly puffed up by his fleshly mind" is also not a bad translation, but it could be tweaked just a bit. It could read: "to no purpose, having a false pride by their earthly nature *(as opposed to their godly spiritual nature)* **of their inner most heart."**

A better translation per the Greek for Colossians 2:18 and the topical context of the various sub-topics expanded in their own studies as mentioned in this verse.

> *Don't let <u>anyone</u> whoever it may be (man or spirit), defraud or deprive you of your heavenly reward <u>from your Christian observance of God's Word</u> by a pretended humility where they (your leadership) are worshipping <u>misleading</u> angels, intruding into those things which they have not seen or understood. To no purpose, having a false pride by their earthly nature (as opposed to their godly spiritual nature) of their inner most heart.*

Ephesians 4:22-24 KJV
22 That ye put off concerning the former conversation the old man, which is corrupt according to the deceitful lusts;
23 And be renewed in the spirit of your mind;
24 And that ye put on the new man, which after God is created in righteousness and true holiness.

Colossians 3:8 KJV
8 But now ye also put off all these; ...
(the things of the earth).

Colossians 3:10 KJV

10 And have put on the new *man*, which is renewed^{G341-V} in knowledge after the image of him that created him:

2 Corinthians 5:17 KJV
17 Therefore if any man be in Christ, he is a new creature: old things are passed away; *(old habits/actions/attitudes)* behold, all things [*that you renewed your mind to*] are become new.

Romans 13:14 KJV
14 But put ye on the Lord Jesus Christ, *(by the renewed mind)* and make not provision for the flesh, *(old habits/actions/attitudes)* to *fulfil* the lusts *thereof.*

Ephesians 6:10-11 KJV
10 Finally, my brethren, be strong in the Lord, and in the power of his might.
11 Put on the whole armour of God, that ye may be able to stand against the wiles of the devil.

Colossians 3:14 KJV
14 And above all these things *put on* *(properly supplied from Col. 3:12 context)* charity, which is the bond of perfectness.

8: Walking in God's Word = Walking in the renewed mind = Walking in God's love

There are several words translated "walk" in the New Testament. I will be concentrating on the Greek word where one of the categories deals with the "regulating or conducting" your Christian lifestyle. This is exactly what the renewed mind does, it helps you change your conduct, not only in your actions, but in your heart *(intentions)* also. This study will add yet another layer to your understanding of what it is to "put-on" the mind of Christ. The title of this chapter is also a mathematical axiom.

If A = B, and B=C, then C=A.
A, B, and C are equal to each other, they just say it in a different way.

A) Walking in God's Word ='s
B) Walking in the Renewed Mind ='s
C) Walking in God's Love

The word "walk" in the Greek is the verb "peripateō" (G4043) which is pronounced "per-ee-pat-eh'-o" and it means: *(I) to walk, to tread or walk about, generally to walk. (II) Figuratively, to live or pass* *one's life, always with an adjunct of manner or circumstances.*[99]

The word **"walk"** in the Greek that we will look at is used in 90 verses with 96 occurrences in the New Testament. There are six verses that have two occurrences of this word. Two of these six verses have the context of physically walking, the other four verses have the context of our walk as a Christian believer. There are two major categories or contexts this word is used in. One is to actually walk, the other is used metaphorically about our lifestyle, our habits. We will also be looking at the two places it is used in which more than two uses are used in a few verses. These are called "clusters" when more than two of the same Greek words are used in a small section of scripture.

8a: RISE, WALK, PRAISING, AND LEAPING

The first pair in the New Testament after the Gospels is in Acts 3:8, but there are more uses in the immediate context making this the first of two clusters we will look at first, a multiple repetition of the same word in just a few verses. A cluster of the

---

[99] Zodhiates, Spiros, Th.D., *(The Complete Word Study Dictionary: New Testament)*, AMG Publishers, Chattanooga, TN., Revised 1993. p. 1148, Ref: 4043, I, II.

same word or derivatives of the root word is a section that God emphasizes over other single use areas. It helps define the word we are looking at, so when we look up the single-use verses or sections, we can apply a general meaning that we have studied from the clustered sections. Verse 8 is the key verse in this cluster because it has two occurrences in it.

> **Acts 3:6-9 KJV**
> **6 Then Peter said, Silver and gold have I none; but such as I have give I thee: In the name of Jesus Christ of Nazareth rise up and walk.**
> **7 And he took him by the right hand, and lifted** *him* **up: and immediately his feet and ankle bones received strength.**
> **8 And he** leaping up stood, and walked, **and entered with them into the temple,** walking, and leaping, and praising God.
> **9 And all the people saw him** walking and praising God**:**

There are a few phrases that connect the word "walk" with another word or clause together with the word "and" that show us where the emphasis is for us to glean from this section.

1. **"rise and walk,"** *(Acts 3:7)*
2. **"leaping up, stood and walked,"** *(Acts 3:8)*
3. **"walking and leaping and praising,"** *(Acts 3:8)*
4. **"walking and praising God."** *(Acts 3:9)*

The first two uses in this section *(Acts 3:7, 8a)* show us his healing being administered. The last two uses *(Acts 3:8b, 9)* show the man praising God for the healing.

The connection to the renewed mind, or living God's Word, or walking in God's love is all in this section. The man was there *(as their custom was for those that had disabilities)* to ask for money so he could buy food etc. But Peter and John got revelation to minister to him, and remembering what Jesus Christ said to them: "freely you have received, freely you should give," they were ready and willing to help with the power from God that was given to them when they were born-again. Peter and John were acting on their renewed mind to live God's Word in their walk with God. They were acting out of God's love in their heart to help others.

Peter gave the man an instruction to rise and walk, and then took his hand to help him up. In verses 4, 6, and 7, Peter operated 4 of the 9 manifestations so the man could be delivered. The man also had to believe he could do it, he had to change his mind and act on what Peter said he could do. After the man started to act with Peter's help, *(by Peter receiving a Word of Wisdom to help)*, God went to work and healed whatever was needed so the man could walk. If the man decided not to stand up with Peter's help, he would have not seen the healing. The man had to make a choice to act on what Peter said before he would be healed, or he could keep looking at his disability and not even try. He had a choice; believe God's word and will for him from Peter, or look at his worldly knowledge from being disabled. The man choose to change his mind to do God's will in his life by listening and following through with allowing Peter to help him. The result was twofold: he was healed, and God got the praise!

The next cluster we will look at is in the Gospel of John where the word has 17 occurrences, the largest number of occurrences in the New Testament. There is a cluster of 4 uses in this Gospel.

> **John 5:5-12 KJV**
> **5** And a certain man was there, which had an infirmity thirty and eight years.
> **6** When Jesus saw him lie, and knew that he had been now a long time *in that case*, he saith unto him, Wilt thou be made whole?
> **7** The impotent man answered him, Sir, I have no man, when the water is

troubled, to put me into the pool: but while I am coming, another steppeth down before me.

8 Jesus saith unto him, Rise, take up thy bed, and walk.

9 And immediately the man was made whole, and took up his bed, and walked: and on the same day was the sabbath.

10 The Jews therefore said unto him that was cured, It is the sabbath day: it is not lawful for thee to carry *thy* bed.

11 He answered them, He that made me whole, the same said unto me, Take up thy bed, and walk.

12 Then asked they him, What man is that which said unto thee, Take up thy bed, and walk?

Jesus Christ was at a place where those that were sick or disabled came to be healed when the water was moved. Jesus Christ was ready and willing to get involved and minister to anyone with a need. He saw a man that could not walk and knew this man was in that condition for many years. Jesus Christ asked the man if he wanted to be healed. This is different from the healing that Peter and John did in that here, Jesus Christ asked the man if he wanted to be healed. *(Was Jesus Christ establishing the man was ready and believing to be healed? I don't know.)* But Peter and John didn't ask. *(Why? Did God show them this man was already believing?)* They demanded the man stand and walk as Peter helped.

> *Each ministering incident is different in how you approach it. Neither one was wrong, both men were healed. Don't get locked in some kind of "ministering" routine where you always have a "set" of things you say in a certain order, or you have a "set" of procedures you follow without any variance. Allow any inspiration or revelation you have guide you on what you need to say and do.*

This is living God's Word in the real world where others need to be healed and you are ready and willing to get involved regardless of the religious leaders of the community that oppose you because you may make them look bad and powerless. And again, we see each man needed to be healed and needed to change their mind and carrying out what Jesus Christ or Peter had demanded from them to be healed.

Each man had to make a choice, the same choice everyone needs to make when they want to see God's Word come to pass in their life. The choice to believe and act on what God's will is for them, or to look at their predicament and not believe there is a way out, even though they have been given a way out through believing in God's power.

8b: WALKING IN DARKNESS, WALKING IN THE LIGHT

The next verse we will look at is John 12:35 because it shows us one of verses where the Greek word is used two times in the context of living His word in our lifestyles. Jesus Christ is encouraging those around him to "walk" in the light *(or truth)* while the light is still available, so that no darkness can come unto them. He also encouraged them to believe in the light *(or truth)* so they could become the children of light. He encouraged them to renew their minds *(thoughts)* to live the truth of God's Word, and that would help keep out the darkness of living without God's Word. It is always a choice between **walking in the light** and **waking in the darkness.** This verse is talking about **spiritual matters, spiritual truth vs. spiritual lies,** and encouraging people to choose to **walk by the spiritual truth** while they still have it available to them.

Here are some verses showing the contrast of **walking in darkness and walking in the light.** This is talking about **spiritual light** or **spiritual darkness.** Another way to say it is **walking by the light of God's Word,** or **walking by darkness of the schemes of this world.**

John 12:35-36 KJV

35 Then Jesus said unto them, Yet a little while is the light with you. Walk while ye have the light, lest darkness come upon you: for he that walketh in darkness knoweth not whither he goeth.
36 While ye have light, believe in the light, that ye may be the children of light. These things spake Jesus, and departed, and did hide himself from them.

John 8:12 KJV
12 Then spake Jesus again unto them, saying, I am the light of the world: he that followeth me shall not walk in darkness, but shall have the light of life.

John 11:9-10 KJV
9 Jesus answered, Are there not twelve hours in the day? If any man walk in the day, he stumbleth not, because he seeth the light of this world.
10 But if a man walk in the night, he stumbleth, because there is no light in him.

The next related verse that has two uses of this Greek word is in Ephesians 4:17. But, I want to show how it sits between two topics that will add to our understanding. The first topic is about living by the schemes of the world, or "every wind of doctrine," that separates and divides people from the true rightly divided Word of God. This can be in the form of the many religious doctrines that have differing interpretations of the Bible, to non-religious belief systems that don't believe in God, but in "inner-humanity" instead to achieve peace and perfection. Both are rooted in the "schemes of the world" to distract you from realizing that it is in rightly dividing God's Word where you find true peace and perfection.

The other topic is about "renewing your mind" to live by God's Word, not by the "schemes of the world." This is hinted at in Ephesians 4:15, but is fully disclosed in Ephesians 4:20-32. The two topics are in conflict with each other, they are mentioning the two choices you have to make each moment. These two areas have always been our choice from the beginning: Do we live by the "schemes of the world," or do we live by God's will for us, as mentioned in His Word? First, Ephesians 4:17.

Ephesians 4:17 KJV
17 This I say therefore, and testify in the Lord, that ye henceforth walk not as other Gentiles walk, in the vanity of their mind,

Verse 17 starts with **"therefore,"** so, what is the "therefore" there for? We will need to read the previous verse to give us the "why" of verse 17. We are not to "walk" *(have a lifestyle)* like the Gentiles *(unbelievers biblically)* because of the truth in verses 14-16!

> **Ephesians 4:14-17 KJV**
> 14 That we *henceforth* <u>be no more children, tossed to and fro, and carried about with every wind of doctrine</u>, by the sleight of men, *and* cunning craftiness, whereby they lie in wait to deceive;
> 15 But speaking the truth in love, may grow up into him in all things, which is the head, *even* Christ:
> 16 From whom the whole body fitly joined together and compacted by that which every joint supplieth, according to the effectual working in the measure of every part, maketh increase of the body unto the edifying of itself in love.
> 17 This I say therefore, and testify in the Lord, that ye henceforth walk <u>not as other Gentiles</u> walk, <u>in the vanity of their mind,</u>

Because of what God did for us by making us a part of "the one body in Christ," we are not to live by our old lifestyle as the Gentiles *(unbelievers)* live. The "one body" is a really big deal today, it is a large part of the "mystery" that was kept secret from before the creation. And in verse 14 and 17 we are given two main areas we are not to adhere to.

1. **Not to be tossed or influenced by "every wind of doctrine," or other belief systems that are not based on the truth of God's Word.** You can have a belief system based on God's Word, but it may be based on "private interpretation" of just a few verses from the truth presented in God's Word. *(Verse 14)*
2. **Not to have a lifestyle based on vanity, ego, selfishness, and pride.** *(Verse 17)*

Instead we are to:
- Speak the truth in love, so we can grow up in the one body and edify each other in God's love. *(Verse 15)*

Verse 15 is the pivot verse regarding what we do with our minds and lifestyles to replace the worldly lifestyle mentioned in verses 14 and 17.

> **Ephesians 4:15 KJV**
> **15 But speaking the truth in love, may grow up into him in all things, which is the head,** *even* **Christ:**

If we continue reading Ephesians 4, we will see how

to carry out Ephesians 4:15, the renewed mind choice we can make so God's will for our lives come to pass. Ephesians 4:20-32.... But here is a summary within this section.

> **Ephesians 4:22-24 KJV**
> **22 That ye put off concerning the former conversation the old man, which is corrupt according to the deceitful lusts;**
> **23 And be renewed in the spirit** *(life)*[100] **of your mind;**
> **24 And that ye put on the new man, which after God is created in righteousness and true holiness.**

These three verses show us how to make the right choice so we can live in God's love. There are two actions we need to take. Praying for God to do these actions for you **is not** taking on your responsibility, but it is setting yourself up for failure and a reason to blame God for not taking away your sin nature. Using an excuse like: "Well, it must not God's will to stop this quite yet." **NO!** You have already read God's will, now **YOU DO IT!**

---

[100] Wierwille, V.P., *(Receiving the holy spirit today)*, American Christian Press, New Knoxville, Ohio 1982. p. Appendix II: 238, Appendix III: 286.

Ephesians 4:22 KJV

22 That ye *(YOU)* **put off** concerning the former conversation the old man, which is corrupt according to the deceitful lusts;

Ephesians 4:24 KJV

24 And that ye *(YOU)* **put on** the new man, which after God is created in righteousness and true holiness.

Do you see the large print above? Can that be made any clearer? Who is responsible to **STOP** the old unrighteous habits? Is it God, or you? Read the verses again, it says YOU *(ye = you in Old or Kings English in the KJV)*.

STOP PRAYING FOR GOD TO TAKE AWAY YOUR SIN! YOU STOP SINNING, YOU TAKE IT AWAY! HOW?

Ephesians 4:24 KJV

24 And that ye *(YOU)* put on the new man, which after God is created in righteousness and true holiness.

YOU PUT ON THE NEW MAN, you change your habits to reflect what God has created in you. That is, Christ in you. Would the Christ in you lie? No, so you speak the truth in any situation. That is **HOW** you stop lying! Would the Christ in you steal? No, so you work a job that meets your needs and any extra can be given to those that have a need. That is **HOW** you stop stealing. **STOP** asking God to take away your ungodly habits, **YOU** stop acting that way by **YOU** replacing your bad actions with good godly actions.

You replace the old habit with a new godly habit that reflects "What would the Christ in you do." The epistles are loaded with replacement habits for our ungodly habits. Ephesians 4:17-32 is one notable example of these chapters. A substantial portion of the epistles contain dozens of comparisons of "bad habits to good habits" centered on walking and living like Jesus Christ. Here are a few sections for example. But many bad habits or wrong habits are also discussed in a discussion style of reproof instead of a "don't do this but do this instead" like in Ephesians 4:24-32. I suggest you take a break from this chapter to read and reread these sections I have mentioned. There are more sections like these that hit on all kinds of topics and attitudes, these are just a sampling so you can understand that these sections are bringing to light lifestyles that are against God's Word with the needed corrections to replace the old habits.

- Romans 12:9-21 *(qualities of a true Christian compared to old habits)*.
- Romans 13:1-7 *(respecting leadership in the Church)*.
- Romans 8:8-14 *(live honestly towards others)*
- 1st Corinthians 3:1-23 *(don't get caught up in self-endorsement or respect of persons)*.
- 1st Corinthians 4:1-21 *(don't think or have an attitude above what is written, listen to your leadership as fathers to their children. True leaders are faithful, and exercise God's power and love)*.
- 1st Corinthians 5:1-13 *(don't hangout or have a relationship with those that are without God, you have a need to witness to them, but not to be friends or partners or supporters with them. We are instructed not to <u>keep company</u> (deeper than just mingling, more intimate) with those wicked persons.*

8c: ENCOURAGEMENT: TALK THE WALK; WALK THE TALK

The next verse we will look at in which the Greek word for "walk" is used two times is 1st John 2:6. But I want to show you the context first. The context is "you need to walk the talk," otherwise you are a liar, and God's truth is not living in you.

1 John 2:3-6 KJV
3 And hereby we do know **that we** know **him, if we** keep **his commandments.**
4 He that saith**, I** know **him, and** keepeth **not his commandments, is a liar, and the truth is not in him.**
5 But whoso keepeth **his word, in him verily is the love of God perfected: hereby** know **we that we are in him.**
6 He that saith **he abideth in him ought himself also so to** walk**, even as he** walked**.**

Okay, we have a lot to look at here. I have given three various kinds of shadings in these verses. All are repetitions, and all teach us **HOW** to live God's Word instead of just putting on an outward appearance of being a true Christian, but without "living by example" like a true Christian. This is the context in this section, and being in 1st John, which is all about maintaining your **relationship, your fellowship** with God makes perfect sense to bring up this "fake Christian" scenario.

Let's look at the four repetitions I have marked above and see how they all keep us on the right track to rightly divide this section. When you see many repetitions of different words in a small section of verses, many times the largest repetition will be become the main topic of these verses. I have listed the four repetitions in the order of the largest to the smaller usage. Notice the word **"know"**[101] is used four times, and it is a verb in the Greek, so this is knowledge that is learned, so you must live it by experience.

This is the main thrust of these verses, to **"know through experience"** this fellowship we can have with God and Jesus Christ. The words **"keep" and "walk"** are the **HOW** to learn about this experience, this fellowship or relationship. The phrase **"He that saith"** gives us our two choices we must do in order to "have" or "not have" that relationship with God and Jesus Christ.

1. **Know 4x:** *to learn to know; this can only be by experience (the learning experience). The result: his love is perfected in us.*
2. **Keep 3x:** *keep His commandments 2x, not keep His commandments 1x*
3. **Walk 2x:** *you should abide in him, as he walked*
4. **He that said 2x:** *bookend, our choices: to walk, or not to walk*

I want to look at 1st John 2:6 now because it has our key word for study in this chapter.

---

[101] Meyers, Rick, (*Thayer's Greek Lexicon Dictionary*) E-Sword Software Version 11.1.0, Copyright ©2000-2017. Ref: G1097, Verb: Def: *1) to learn to know, come to know, get a knowledge of perceive, feel*

1 John 2:6 KJV
6 He that saith he abideth in him ought himself also so to walk, even as he walked.

This is a simple reproof and correction to those who **say** they abide him *(Jesus Christ)*. They should also walk as he walked. In other words, **walk the talk!** This could very easily be a summery of 1st John 2:1-5. Considering the tone of this section, it is obvious that the Apostle John was confronting those that were **bragging how "Christian" they are,** but when it came down to putting Christian principles into practice, they always denied those that need understanding and forgiveness, or God's love. Many so-called Christians are still acting this way. They profess being a Christian, but condemn or wrongly judge others as they double down on the legality of their "religious dogma," but deny them God's judgement, mercy, and faith *(the spirit of Christianity)*.

> *This is one example how some **"put-on" the appearance of being a Christian**. But it is all for "appearance for acceptance sake" and is not genuine Christianity because they don't **walk the talk**. They just talk, that's all, like an empty ceremonial container, pretty on the outside, but empty on the inside.*

The psychology that can be taught from God's Word has always interested me, this section shows a mental attitude with a corresponding action *(or in-*

action), This section reflects what Jesus Christ said about the Pharisees having an appearance of godliness by carrying out the legal aspects of the law, but not the spirit of the law, by not showing God's love. They denied the people "*honest* judgement, mercy, and faith."[102] I believe there are similarities in the psychology of the Pharisees and in those "Christians" that profess following Jesus Christ but deny the spirit of showing God's love in a time of need. They demonstrate **all talk, but no action when really needed.** This verse admonishes all Christians to not only **talk the walk,** but that all Christians should also **walk the talk.** That is a genuine Christian lifestyle in practice. It takes controlling our thoughts to act on what we know we should do to help others to show them God's judgement, mercy, and faith in kindness.

8d: HOW TO: TALK THE WALK AND WALK THE TALK

The next repetition we will look at is the word "keep" which is used three times. This begins our

---

[102] Matthew 23:23, 27 KJV
23 Woe unto you, scribes and Pharisees, hypocrites! for ye pay tithe of mint and anise and cummin, and have omitted the weightier *matters* of the law, judgment, mercy, and faith: these ought ye to have done, and not to leave the other undone.
27 Woe unto you, scribes and Pharisees, hypocrites! for ye are like unto whited sepulchres, which indeed appear beautiful outward, but are within full of dead *men's* bones, and of all uncleanness.

study in this section that will start to show us **how** to walk the talk.

> 1 John 2:3-5 KJV
> 3 And hereby we do know that we know him, if we keep his commandments.
> 4 He that saith, I know him, and keepeth not his commandments, is a liar, and the truth is not in him.
> 5 But whoso keepeth his word, in him verily is the love of God perfected: hereby know we that we are in him.

The first thing I like to do with repetitions is to observe any similarities and comparisons of the clauses in which the word is repeated in. So, my first observation is that there is one negative use *(verse 4: keep **not** his commandments),* and two positive uses. *(verse 3b: keep his commandments, 5a: keepeth his word).*

The second observation is that two uses are connected with the word "**commandments**" and one use is connected with word, "**word**" *(referring to the commandments)* shown in my first observation. And the other connected word is the word **"know,"** used three times in two verses which tell us that to **"keep"** His commandments is also to **"know"** *(by experience)* His commandments. One could also understand it like this: **To know His commandments by** experience is to actually live His commandments by changing our thoughts and actions to keep and do God's Word. Otherwise, we are not walking the talk, and you are a liars because the truth is not living in us.

The third observation is that the results or status of the person who **doesn't keep** the commandments differs from those that do. *(Verse 4d: is a liar, and the truth is not in him 5b: in him verily is the love of God perfected).*

The forth observation is that verses 3 and 5 complement each other. *(Verse 3: we know that we know him if we keep his commandments, and verse 5: if we keep his word, God's love is perfected in us, and we know we are in him).*

Here is another way to look at it in an outline form. Look at the results *(or outcome)* of each.

1. Keep:
    a. His commandments 2x *(topic)*
    b. Commandments 2x *(connected word)*
    c. Word 1x *(connected word)*
    d. In him is the love of God is perfected *(result)*
    e. We know we are in him because we live His commandments 2x *(result)*
2. Not Keep:

    a. His commandments 1x *(topic)*
    b. We don't keep His commandments, though we say, "we know Him." We are a liar *(result)*
    c. The truth is not in us *(result)*

So, we see the results of **keeping, and not keeping His Word.** Now I want to bring up one more repetition in this section that gets to the psychological part of this section. The phrase **"he that saith"** shows us the choice a person must make: to do, or not to do God's Word. This phrase is a special kind of repetition, it is used to block off a section, nick-named a "bookend."[103] So we pay attention to not only the repeated phrase, but we also pay attention to what is said between the repeated phrase and understand that the "in between" matter is related to the repeated phrase. That is, the things said between the repeated phrases helps to explain more of the details regarding the repetition.

The fascinating thing about this repetition is that it puts emphasis on the two choices we have along with the outcome of each. God has always given us a choice to do or not to do His Word from the

---

[103] Nessle, Jon O., *(Repetitions-Revealing a Hidden Key to the Heart of Scripture)*, Next Reformation Publishing Co. Plainfield, https://www.academia.edu/24932331/Repetitions_A_Key_to_Understanding_the_Heart_of_Scripture

beginning. And here we see it again, encouragement to do His Word so we can have a good outcome.

> **1 John 2:4-6 KJV**
> **4 He that saith, I know him, and keepeth not his commandments, is a liar, and the truth is not in him.**
> 5 But whoso keepeth his word, in him verily is the love of God perfected: hereby know we that we are in him.
> **6 He that saith he abideth in him ought himself also so to walk, even as he walked.**

He that saith:
1. ... I know him and does not keep his commandments is a liar... *(Verse 4)*
2. ... I abide in him, then they should also walk as he walked *(Verse 6)*

Do you see how the verses with this "bookend" repetition shows us the negative side of our possible choice with the result? And verse 5 *(in between this "bookend")*[104] gives us the positive side of our possible choice with the result.

---

[104] Bullinger, E.W. *(Figures of Speech used in the Bible)*, Baker Book House, Grand Rapids, Michigan.16th printing 1991. p. 199 **"Anaphora or like sentence beginnings,"** also can qualify for p. 245 **"Epanadiplosis or Encircling."**

1. Who soever keeps His commandments, God's love is perfected in him.

Another way to look at these three verses is if you choose to live like 1st John 2:4 states, then you have **decided <u>not</u> to do** God's Word but yet **you profess to do** God's Word, so you are a liar and God's Word does not live in you. Does this remind you of any "professed Christians" you have met? They are also the first to wrongly judge and condemn others without knowing all the facts. They **"act"** Christian in public and in private **until** they find a fault in you, and then you are shunned and publicly called out! There is no forgiveness or compassion in them. You are humiliated and left to self-condemnation and anger.

In today's categorizing of different types of Christianity, these groups are referred to as the right-leaning Christians, who have a very legalistic theology of conduct, without any room for error. They talk about God's love, mercy *(forgiveness)*, and righteous judgement, but don't offer it to those who need it most. Instead, they reject people and condemn them because they did not conduct themselves according to a false standard of Christianity. This is the type of person **"professing"** to be a Christian but not living God's Word as 1st John 2:4 states. The Word of God says they are liars and His Word does not live in them.

In 1st John 2:5 we see the other choice we have concerning God's Word in our lives. This choice is to **"keep"** God's Word so that God's love is perfected in us. This implies **"doing"** His Word, that is, living God's Word, *(the word **know** cooperates this also)*. I want you to notice that I have shaded three words below in 1st John 2:5, all are verbs! Verbs are **"DOING"** words, they demand action on your part. The word **"keepeth"** is key to understanding this verse. I believe it is used figuratively here because the base meaning means to "watch," or "observe," or "guard." Remember this is a verb, so action is involved, this is not a passive verb, but an active verb.

Figuratively it can mean to "obey," to "fulfil a duty or task," or "to perform watchfully." If you look up this word in the Greek, you will notice that this word has you **doing** something that causes you to guard or observe that thing. A connecting word is the word **"do"** (when you do a word study of **"keep"** in the Greek).

> **1 John 2:5 KJV**
> **5 But whoso keepeth**(verb) **his word, in him verily is the love of God perfected:** (verb) **hereby know**(verb) **we that we are in him.**

The word "keepeth" in 1ˢᵗ John 2:5 is the Greek verb "tēreō" (G5083) which is pronounced "tay-reh'-o" and it means: *a warden, guard. To keep an eye on, watch, and hence to guard, keep, obey.... (I) ... figuratively, to obey, observe, keep, fulfil a duty, precept, law, custom, or custom meaning to preform watchfully, vigilantly.*[105]

You are guarding God's Word in your life when you are doing it *(living it)*. God's love will then grow more and more towards being complete in your life. This is how you will understand that you are indeed living as he *(Jesus Christ)* lived, and that his word lives in you.

After 1ˢᵗ John 2:4-5 shows us our two choices, verse 6 gives us something to consider. It challenges us to **talk the walk, and walk the talk** so we can have the maximum benefit. God won't force us to do His Word, but God has given us a choice. Which choice will you choose? Remember, 1ˢᵗ John 2:6 is one of six verses out of ninety verses that have the word **"walk"** used twice in it. So, God's challenge to **"to talk the walk, and walk the talk"** is set forth for us to consider knowing our options from 1ˢᵗ John 2:4-5.

---

[105] Zodhiates, Spiros, Th.D., *(The Complete Word Study Dictionary: New Testament)*, AMG Publishers, Chattanooga, TN., Revised 1993. p. 1380, Ref: 5083, general definition and (I).

From the beginning, God has wanted us to love each other. Jesus Christ taught the people with this topic as paramount in his teachings and actions.[106] This has been God's commandment from the beginning.

In the last verse that has the word **"walk"** used twice in it, we will see what it is to **"walk in love."** There are many ideas floating around to suggest to us what it is to **"walk in love"** biblically. I like to go to God's Word and let it define what this phrase means with word studies related to the phrase.

8e: WALKING IN GOD'S LOVE = WALKING IN GOD'S WORD = WALKING IN THE RENEWED MIND

Let's look at the context that 2nd John 1:6 is in and work the structure with the multiple repetitions that are present.

I have shaded the four repetitions and double underlined the key phrase in this section that pulls

---

[106] Mark 12:29-31 KJV
29 And Jesus answered him, The first of all the commandments *is,* Hear, O Israel; The Lord our God is one Lord:
30 And thou shalt **love the Lord thy God** with all thy heart, and with all thy soul, and with all thy mind, and with all thy strength: this *is* the first commandment.
31 And the second *is* like, *namely* this, Thou shalt **love thy neighbour** as thyself. There is none other commandment greater than these.

from the surrounding verses and phrases that are given after this explanation. Let me first explain what you will be looking at as far the basic structure of how these repetitions interact.

There are two phrases that have overlapping words in our key phrase in verse 6. The two words are shaded. "And this is love, that we walk after his commandments."

The two phrases that have an overlap in the key phrase in verse 6.

V5d: "... from the beginning, that we love one another."
V6c: "... from the beginning, ye should walk in it."

THE KEY PHASE BETWEEN THE ABOVE TWO SIMILAR PHRASES:
V6a: "And this is love,(V5d) that we walk(V6c) after his commandments."

Putting it all together:

V5d: ... but that which we had **from the beginning**, that we love one another.
6 And this is love, that we walk after his commandments. This is the commandment, That, as

ye have heard **from the beginning,** ye should **walk** in it.

V5d **LOVE** (from the beginning)
V6c **walk** (from the beginning)
V6a LOVE and WALK (from the beginning)

And the word "commandments" *(God's Word)* is connected to BOTH the word **"love,"** and the word **"walk."** To love with God's love is to walk according to *(or after)* God's Word. That involves **renewing your mind** to **keep and do** God's Word. If you want **the love of** *(or from)* **God to grow closer to perfection,** you will need to **renew your mind** to live God's Word, His principles of life. Do you see how God's love and walking according to His Word are interconnected? The only way to have God's love in your life is to **renew your mind** to live His commandments, His Word, there are no exceptions.[107]

Important repetitions show us what is being emphasized. Within these 3 verses are 4 repetitions that set the main topics of this section for proper interpretation. When studying this section knowing what repetitions are prominent, it is important in

---

[107] Nessle, Jon O., *(Jesus' Keys to Life-Foundational Class)* Next Reformation Publishing Co. Plainfield, In.

order to rightly divide this section, to take into account how the repetitions give emphasis to specific topics, and how the rest of the section fits within those topics. Again, I will list them by the number of uses in these verses, larger to smaller. The larger repetition holds a higher authority of importance over smaller repetitions.

2nd John 1:4-6
"commandment" 4x *(main topic)*
"walk" 3x *(secondary topic)*
"from the beginning" 2x *(supporting topic)*
"love" 2x *(supporting topic)*

> **2 John 1:4-6 KJV**
> 4 I rejoiced greatly that I found of thy children walking in truth, as we have received a **commandment** from the Father.
> 5 And now I beseech thee, lady, not as though I wrote a new **commandment** unto thee, but that which we had from the beginning, that we *love* one another.
> 6 And this is *love,* that we walk after his **commandments.** This is the **commandment,** That, as ye have heard from the beginning, ye should walk in it.

I want to show you again two similar repetitions from these verses that show us in another way that we should **"walk the talk and talk the walk."** These phrases that form bookends show us how to carry this out between the bookends.

V5d: "... from the beginning, that we love one another."
V6c: "... from the beginning, ye should walk in it."
HOW?
V6a: "And this is love,**(V5d)** that we walk**(V6c)** after his commandments."

That we should love one another is to walk in God's Word *(we do this by renewing (changing) our thoughts and actions)*. The underlined phrases in v5b and v6c are equal to each other. To love one another **IS TO** walk in God's Word. To live in God's love **IS TO** renew our mind to live God's Word.

It is time to take a deep breath and consider this chapter research in a simpler form. Here is a summery of some of the main points we looked at with verses that contained two uses of the word **"walk"** from the Greek.

- Acts 3:8, main words: **rise, walk, praising, and leaping.** This is talking about a physical healing, but also includes mental praising.

- o For your consideration: We are also to rise-up and walk mentally when it comes to renewing our minds to live God's Word. We will have the same results, we will praise God and leap for joy mentally.

- John 12:35-36, A contrast: **Walking in darkness, walking in the light.** *(our choice we always have)*
  - o Ephesians 4:14-17, **Reveals how:** to **walk in darkness** or how to **walk in the light** from John 12:35-36.

- 1st John 2:3-6, **Talk the walk, walk the talk.**

- 2nd John 1:4-6, **Walking in God's love = walking In God's Word = walking in the renewed mind.**

We have looked at only a few verses that have the Greek word translated **"walk"** or variations of it, to point out some basic principles about what the renewed mind is and how it works. The Gospel of John contains the most uses of this word in any one chapter or book. If you want to know how to **walk as a son of God**, with God's love evident in your life, reading the Gospel of John will show you how Jesus Christ **talked the walk and walked the talk** of living in God's love by keeping his mind renewed to his Fathers word in all the choices he made as he was confronted with everyday challenges. Here are a few more verses from this word study for further research. Be sure to read the surrounding context these verses are placed in for a fuller understanding.

> **Romans 6:4-5 KJV**
> **4 Therefore we are buried with him by baptism into death: that like as Christ was raised up from the dead by the glory of the Father, even so we also should walk in newness of life.**
> **5 For if we have been planted together in the likeness of his death, we shall be also** *in the likeness* **of** *his* **resurrection:**

Because we have the hope of being raised from the dead with the same spiritual body Jesus Christ has now, we should choose to walk in our newness of life we have through our gift of holy spirit. This is done by putting on the life principles found in God's Word.

> **Romans 8:4-6 KJV**
> **4 That the righteousness of the law might be fulfilled in us, who walk not after the flesh, but [walk] after the Spirit.**
> **5 For they that are after the flesh do mind the things of the flesh; but they that are after the Spirit the things of the Spirit.**

6 For to be carnally minded *is* death; but to be spiritually minded *is* life and peace.

To walk after the spirit is to be spiritually minded which is life. To walk after the flesh *(figuratively meaning by your five senses, without consulting God through your gift of holy spirit)* is to be carnally minded which is death.

2 Corinthians 5:7 KJV
7 (For we walk by faith, not by sight:)

When we are walking by the spirit, we are walking by our believing, not by our five senses.

Galatians 5:16 KJV
16 *This* I say then, Walk in the Spirit, and ye shall not fulfil the lust of the flesh.

You can't **walk by the spirit** and fulfil the desires of sense-knowledge at the same time. We can either make decisions by the spirit, or we can make decisions by the flesh *(limited by the five senses)*. It is a choice we make every day, many times a day.

Ephesians 2:8,10 KJV
8 For by grace are ye saved through faith; and that not of yourselves: *it is* the

gift of God:
10 For we are his workmanship, created in Christ Jesus unto good works, which God hath before ordained that we should walk in them.

Ephesians 4:1 KJV
1 I therefore, the prisoner of the Lord, beseech you that ye walk worthy of the vocation wherewith ye are called,

God has created His spirit in us, we are His masterpiece in Christ unto good works. We should walk in those good works.

Colossians 1:10 KJV
10 That ye might walk worthy of the Lord unto all pleasing, being fruitful in every good work, and increasing in the knowledge of God;

Part of walking worthy is increasing in the knowledge from God. This is a complete acknowledgment of God's Word, that is, applying it by renewing our minds to the end we fully understand His Word.

Colossians 2:6-7 KJV
6 As ye have therefore received Christ Jesus the Lord, *so* walk ye in him:

7 Rooted and built up in him, and stablished in the faith, as ye have been taught, abounding therein with thanksgiving.

Verse 7 is your goal for this book! To become **ROOTED, BUILT UP, and ESTABLISHED in the faith.** What kind of faith? The Family Faith, The One Body, where all believers are contributing their best so we can help the believers, so we can operate without divisions, so the church is built up to meet everyone's needs as they come up. And we are to be thankful.

> **2 John 1:6 KJV**
> **6 And this is <u>love,</u> that we walk after his commandments. This is the commandment, That, as ye have heard from the beginning, ye should walk in it.**
>
> **1 Corinthians 13:13 KJV**
> **13 And now abideth faith, hope, charity,** *(love)* **these three; but the greatest of these** *is* **charity.** *(love)*

Confirm Your Calling as the Elect of God

2 Peter 1:1-8 KJV

1 Simon Peter, a servant and an apostle of Jesus Christ, to them that have obtained like precious faith with us through the righteousness of God and our Saviour Jesus Christ:

2 Grace and peace be multiplied unto you through the knowledge of God, and of Jesus our Lord,

3 According as his divine power hath given unto us all things that *pertain* unto life and godliness, through the knowledge of him that hath called us to glory and virtue:

4 Whereby are given unto us exceeding great and precious promises: that by these ye might be partakers of the divine nature, having escaped the corruption that is in the world through lust.

5 And beside this, giving all diligence, **add**[108] to your faith virtue; and to virtue [*add*] knowledge;

---

[108] Bullinger, E.W. *(Figures of Speech used in the Bible)*, Baker Book House, Grand Rapids, Michigan.16th printing 1991. p. 70, ref: C: **The Ellipsis of Repetition:** Where the omitted word or words is, or are to be supplied out

6 And to knowledge *[add]* **temperance; and to temperance** *[add]* **patience; and to patience** *[add]* **godliness;**
7 And to godliness *[add]* **brotherly kindness; and to brotherly kindness** *[add]* **charity.**
8 For if these things be in you, *(verses 5-7),* and abound, *[then]* they make *you that ye shall* neither *be* barren nor unfruitful in the knowledge of our Lord Jesus Christ.

This is the renewed mind in a summary that shows us the greatness of what is available when we **keep and do** the precepts from God's Word.

There is a repetition that sets this section on fire concerning the proper interpretation. In 2nd Peter 1:2b and 3b *(shaded above)* the phrase **"through the knowledge of God and Jesus Christ/Him"** box in the clause in verse 3: **"According as his divine power hath given unto us all things that** *pertain* **unto life and godliness."** We have been given "all things unto life and godliness" in the applied knowledge of the precepts from God's Word, as we change our thoughts and habits to walk in His commandments.

---

of the *preceding* or *following* clause, in order to compete the sense. This is a simple ellipsis

The word "knowledge" in 2nd Peter 1:2-3 is the Greek noun "epignōsis" (G1922) which is pronounced "ip-ig'-no-sis." which means: *It is more than "gnōsis" (G1108) knowledge, because it expresses a more thorough participation in the acquiring of knowledge on the part of the learner. ... a knowledge laying claim to personal involvement.*[109]

2nd Peter 1:8 is my believing for you to have in your life as you apply the Word of God in areas you need to change and form new habits that will glorify God and bless you with His promises to you.

Here is the list from verses 5-7 that the Apostle Peter encourages us to add to our habits and mindset so we can be successful powerful Christians.

1. To Believing, **add**
2. Virtue, to virtue **add**
3. Knowledge, to knowledge **add**
4. Temperance, to temperance **add**
5. Patience, to patience **add**
6. Godliness, to godliness **add**
7. Brotherly Kindness, to brotherly kindness **add**
8. Charity. *(God's love)*

---

[109] Zodhiates, Spiros, Th.D., *(The Complete Word Study Dictionary: New Testament)*, AMG Publishers, Chattanooga, TN., Revised 1993. p. 624, Ref: 1922, general definition.

The list is in an intentional, numeric order having spiritual significance. For example, believing is first, and the number one means *a symbol of unity, it denotes in God there is sufficiency, it marks the beginning.*[110] Believing relies on God to supply what we are believing for. Believing Romans 10:9-10 is our beginning of our new Christian lifestyle, God supplies us His gift of holy spirit at that time.

> Colossians 3:1-17 KJV
> 1 If ye then be risen with Christ, seek those things which are above, where Christ sitteth on the right hand of God.
> 2 Set your affection *(thoughts and actions)* on things above, not on things on the earth.
> 3 For ye are dead, and your life is hid with Christ in God.
> 4 When Christ, *who is* our life, shall appear, then shall ye also appear with him in glory.
> 5 Mortify therefore your members which are upon the earth; fornication, uncleanness, inordinate affection, evil concupiscence, and covetousness, which is idolatry:

---

[110] Bullinger, E.W. *(Number in Scripture),* Kregel Publications, Grand Rapids, MI. Part II: Spiritual Significance. p. 50-282

6 For which things' sake the wrath of God cometh on the children of disobedience:
7 In the which ye also walked some time, when ye lived in them.
8 But now ye also put off all these; anger, wrath, malice, blasphemy, filthy communication out of your mouth.
9 Lie not one to another, seeing that ye have put off the old man with his deeds;
10 And have put on the new *man*, which is renewed in knowledge after the image of him that created him:
11 Where there is neither Greek nor Jew, circumcision nor uncircumcision, Barbarian, Scythian, bond *nor* free: but Christ *is* all, and in all.
12 Put on therefore, as the elect of God, holy and beloved, bowels of mercies, kindness, humbleness of mind, meekness, longsuffering;
13 Forbearing one another, and forgiving one another, if any man have a quarrel against any: even as Christ forgave you, so also *do* ye.
14 And above all these things *put on* charity, which is the bond of perfectness.
15 And let the peace of God rule in your hearts, to the which also ye are called in one body; and be ye thankful.

16 Let the word of Christ dwell in you richly in all wisdom; teaching and admonishing one another in psalms and hymns and spiritual songs, singing with grace in your hearts to the Lord.
17 And whatsoever ye do in word or deed, *do* all in the name of the Lord Jesus, giving thanks to God and the Father by him.

Proverbs 4:10-18 KJV
10 Hear, O my son, and receive my sayings; and the years of thy life shall be many.
11 I have taught thee in the way of wisdom; I have led thee in right paths.
12 When thou goest, thy steps shall not be straitened; and when thou runnest, thou shalt not stumble.
13 Take fast hold of instruction; let *her* not go: keep her; for she *is* thy life.
14 Enter not into the path of the wicked, and go not in the way of evil *men*.
15 Avoid it, pass not by it, turn from it, and pass away.
16 For they sleep not, except they have done mischief; and their sleep is taken away, unless they cause *some* to fall.
17 For they eat the bread of wickedness, and drink the wine of violence.

18 But the path of the just *is* as the shining light, that shineth more and more unto the perfect day.

1 John 4:7-17 KJV
7 Beloved, let us love one another: for love is of God; and every one that loveth is born of God, and knoweth God.
8 He that loveth not knoweth not God; for God is love.
9 In this was manifested the love of God toward us, because that God sent his only begotten Son into the world, that we might live through him.
10 Herein is love, not that we loved God, but that he loved us, and sent his Son *to be* the propitiation for our sins.
11 Beloved, if God so loved us, we ought also to love one another.
12 No man hath seen God at any time. If we love one another, God dwelleth in us, and his love is perfected in us.
13 Hereby know we that we dwell in him, and he in us, because he hath given us of his Spirit.
14 And we have seen and do testify that the Father sent the Son *to be* the Saviour of the world.
15 Whosoever shall confess that Jesus is the Son of God, God dwelleth in him, and he in God.

16 And we have known and believed the love that God hath to us. God is love; and he that dwelleth in love dwelleth in God, and God in him.
17 Herein is our love made perfect, that we may have boldness in the day of judgment: because as he is, so are we in this world.

1 John 4:18-21 KJV
18 There is no fear in love; but perfect love casteth out fear: because fear hath torment. He that feareth is not made perfect in love.
19 We love him, because he first loved us.
20 If a man say, I love God, and hateth his brother, he is a liar: for he that loveth not his brother whom he hath seen, how can he love God whom he hath not seen?
21 And this commandment have we from him, That he who loveth God love his brother also.

God Bless You, and Peace and Grace from God your Father and from His son Jesus Christ.

Works Cited

Arbib, Peter., *(20+ Benefits Speaking in Tongues Has for You)*, Sound Wisdom Publications, Camby, IN. 2018

Arbib, Peter., *(Can I Really Speaking in Tongues?)*, Sound Wisdom Publications, Camby, IN. 2017

Aykin, Nuray, *(Pomegranates and Grapes)*, iUniverse, 2012, Photo Credit via Thinkstock

Bullinger, E.W. *(Figures of Speech used in the Bible)*, Baker Book House, Grand Rapids, Michigan. 16th printing 1991.

Bullinger, E.W. *(The Companion Bible)*, Zondervan Bible Publishers, Grand Rapids, Michigan.

Bullinger, E.W. *(Number in Scripture)*, Kregel Publications, Grand Rapids, MI.

Bullinger, E.W. *(Word Studies of the Holy Spirit)*, Kregel Publications, Grand Rapids, MI.

Clapp, Wayne., *(Ready and Willing)*, Christian Family Fellowship, Tipp City, Ohio.

Gesenius, H.W.F., *(Genesius' Hebrew-Chaldee Lexicon to the Old Testament)*, Baker Books House Company, Grand Rapids, MI. ©1979.

Meyers, Rick, (*Brown-Driver-Briggs Hebrew Dictionary*) E-Sword Software Version 11.1.0, Copyright ©2000-2017.

Meyers, Rick, (*John Westley Commentary*), E-Sword Software Version 11.1.0, Copyright ©2000-2017

Meyers, Rick, (*Strong's Hebrew and Greek Dictionary*) E-Sword Software Version 11.1.0, Copyright ©2000-2017

Meyers, Rick, (*Thayer's Greek Lexicon Dictionary*) E-Sword Software Version 11.1.0, Copyright ©2000-2017

Nessle, Jon O., (*Jesus' Keys to Life-Foundational Class*) Next Reformation Publishing Co. Plainfield, In.

Nessle, Jon O., (*Repetitions-Revealing a Hidden Key to the Heart of Scripture*), Next Reformation Publishing Co. Plainfield, https://www.academia.edu/24932331/Repetitions_A_Key_to_Understanding_the_Heart_of_Scripture

Strong, James. *(The New Strong's Exhaustive Concordance of the Bible)*, Thomas Nelson Publishers. 1996.

Thayer, Joseph H., (*Thayer's Greek-English Lexicon of the New Testament*), Baker Books House, Grand Michigan, 24th printing.

Webster's., *(Webster's Encyclopedic Unabridged Dictionary of the English Language)*, Portland House 1997 a division of Random House Value Publishing, NY, New York.

Wierwille, V.P., *(Receiving the Holy Spirit Today)*, American Christian Press, New Knoxville, Ohio 1982

Zodhiates, Spiros, Th.D., *(The Complete Word Study Dictionary: New Testament)*, AMG Publishers, Chattanooga, TN., Revised 1993.

Made in the USA
Monee, IL
01 July 2021